Merry Christmas, Mrs. Remasce

from, Shawn Gribouski

Best Loved
POEMS
To Read
Again & Again

Second Series

Best Loved
POEMS
To Read
Again & Again

Second Series

The Most Moving Verses
in the
English Language

Compiled by
Mary Sanford Laurence

Galahad Books   **New York City**

To Kathleen Roche,
my friendly counterpart,
whose guidance and vision
made this book possible.

Published in 1991 by
Galahad Books
A division of LDAP, Inc.
386 Park Avenue South
New York, NY 10016

Galahad Books is a registered trademark of LDAP, Inc.

Library of Congress Catalog Card Number: 89-84000
ISBN: 0-88365-726-0

Printed in the United States of America

Contents

CREED

DISILLUSIONMENT

ELEGY

ETERNITY

FACING DEATH

LIVE FOR TODAY

LOVE

PATRIOTISM

PEACE

POETRY

PORTRAITS

RENEWAL

ROMANCE

YOUTH

Foreword

Putting one's thoughts into words can sometimes be frustrating. At times, words can become a limitation—we are left thinking how we felt so much more than we were able to convey.

However, words can also challenge us into thinking a new way—pushing the limits of our individual scope and opening us up to a larger world.

Poetry captures in a few words the thoughts and emotions that reach to the heart of human experience, flashing insight on the universal truths that unite all of us. In a unique way, poetry is able to break the boundaries of unspoken feelings, helping the reader feel that he or she is not alone; uniting the reader with the world around him.

The poems in this collection celebrate the variety of beliefs, visions and hopes that we share with others—and sometimes stand alone to defend. In this volume are poems of joy, of love, of faith; poems of sacrifice, truth and romance; poems that celebrate living, tell a story, re-affirm the soul. Many of them will be familiar; many are works by poets you have enjoyed through the years: Walt Whitman, Robert Frost, Amy Lowell, Carl Sandburg, William Wordsworth, Dylan Thomas, Edgar Allan Poe, John Keats, Tennyson, Shakespeare, Shelley, Byron and many more. New poets and poems may be waiting to be discovered. Each is a complete portrait, a painting in words which is framed by your own thoughts, memories and feelings about life. Some you will be able to identify with; some will make you laugh; some will make you think; but all the poems within these pages were chosen because they are the kind of poems that will stay with you, become a part of you—the kind you will want to read again and again. This is a book which you will treasure as a source of beauty, inspiration and renewal for years to come.

Best Loved
POEMS
To Read
Again & Again

Second Series

BEAUTY

She Walks in Beauty

She walks in beauty, like the night
Of cloudless climes and starry skies,
And all that's best of dark and bright
Meet in her aspect and her eyes;
Thus mellowed to that tender light
Which heaven to gaudy day denies.

One shade the more, one ray the less,
Had half impaired the nameless grace
Which waves in every raven tress
Or softly lightens o'er her face,
Where thoughts serenely sweet express
How pure, how dear their dwelling-place.

And on that cheek and o'er that brow
So soft, so calm, yet eloquent,
The smiles that win, the tints that glow
But tell of days in goodness spent,
A mind at peace with all below,
A heart whose love is innocent.

GEORGE GORDON, LORD BYRON

Beauty Is Not Bound

Give beauty all her right!
She's not to one form tied;
Each shape yields fair delight
Where her perfections bide:
Helen, I grant, might pleasing be,
And Rosamond was as sweet as she.

Some the quick eye commends,
Some swelling lips and red;
Pale looks have many friends,
Through sacred sweetness bred:
Meadows have flowers that pleasures move,
Though roses are the flowers of love.

Free beauty is not bound
To one unmovèd clime;
She visits every ground
And favors every time.
Let the old loves with mine compare;
My sovereign is as sweet and fair.

THOMAS CAMPION

Shall I Compare Thee
to a Summer's Day?

Shall I compare thee to a summer's day?
Thou art more lovely and more temperate:
Rough winds do shake the darling buds of May,
And summer's lease hath all too short a date:
Sometime too hot the eye of heaven shines,
And often is his gold complexion dimm'd;
And every fair from fair sometime declines,
By chance, or nature's changing course untrimm'd;
But thy eternal summer shall not fade,
Nor lose possession of that fair thou ow'st,
Nor shall death brag thou wander'st in his shade,
When in eternal lines to time thou grow'st;
   So long as men can breathe, or eyes can see,
   So long lives this, and this gives life to thee.

WILLIAM SHAKESPEARE

Ode on a Grecian Urn

I

Thou still unravish'd bride of quietness.
　　Thou foster-child of silence and slow time,
Sylvan historian, who canst thus express
　　A flowery tale more sweetly than our rhyme:
What leaf-fring'd legend haunts about the shape
　　Of deities or mortals, or of both,
　　　In Tempe or the dales of Arcady?
　　What men or gods are these? What maidens loth?
What mad pursuit? What struggle to escape?
　　What pipes and timbrels? What wild ecstasy?

II

Heard melodies are sweet, but those unheard
　　Are sweeter; therefore, ye soft pipes, play on;
Not to the sensual ear, but, more endear'd,
　　Pipe to the spirit ditties of no tone:
Fair youth, beneath the trees, thou canst not leave
　　Thy song, nor ever can those trees be bare;
　　Bold Lover, never, never canst thou kiss,
Though winning near the goal—yet, do not grieve;
　　She cannot fade, though thou hast not thy bliss,
　　For ever wilt thou love, and she be fair!

III

Ah, happy, happy boughs! that cannot shed
  Your leaves, nor ever bid the Spring adieu;
And, happy melodist, unwearied,
  Forever piping songs forever new;
More happy love! more happy, happy love!
  Forever warm and still to be enjoy'd,
    Forever panting, and forever young;
All breathing human passion far above,
  That leaves a heart high-sorrowful and cloy'd,
    A burning forehead, and a parching tongue.

IV

Who are these coming to the sacrifice?
  To what green altar, O mysterious priest,
Lead'st thou that heifer lowing at the skies,
  And all her silken flanks with garlands drest?
What little town by river or sea shore,
  Or mountain-built with peaceful citadel,
    Is emptied of this folk, this pious morn
And, little town, thy streets for evermore
  Will silent be; and not a soul to tell
    Why thou art desolate, can e'er return.

O Attic shape! Fair attitude! with brede
   Of marble men and maidens overwrought,
With forest branches and the trodden weed;
   Thou, silent form, dost tease us out of thought
As doth eternity: Cold Pastoral!
   When old age shall this generation waste,
   Thou shalt remain, in midst of other woe
Than ours, a friend to man, to whom thou say'st,
   'Beauty is truth, truth beauty,'—that is all
   Ye know on earth, and all ye need to know.

JOHN KEATS

I Am

I am: yet what I am none cares or knows,
    My friends forsake me like a memory lost;
I am the self-consumer of my woes,
    They rise and vanish in oblivious host,
Like shades in love and death's oblivion lost;
And yet I am, and live with shadows tost

Into the nothingness of scorn and noise,
    Into the living sea of waking dreams,
Where there is neither sense of life nor joys,
    But the vast shipwreck of my life's esteems;
And e'en the dearest—that I loved the best—
Are strange—nay, rather stranger than the rest.

I long for scenes where man has never trod;
    A place where woman never smiled or wept;
There to abide with my Creator, God,

And sleep as I in childhood sweetly slept:
Untroubling and untroubled where I lie;
The grass below—above the vaulted sky.

JOHN CLARE

Then Hate Me When Thou Wilt

Then hate me when thou wilt; if ever, now;
Now, while the world is bent my deeds to cross,
Join with the spite of fortune, make me bow,
And do not drop in for an after-loss:
Ah! do not, when my heart hath 'scaped this sorrow,
Come in the rearward of a conquered woe;
Give not a windy night a rainy morrow,
To linger out a purposed overthrow.
If thou wilt leave me, do not leave me last,
When other petty griefs have done their spite,
But in the onset come; so shall I taste
At first the very worst of fortune's might;
   And other strains of woe, which now seem woe,
   Compared with loss of thee will not seem so.

WILLIAM SHAKESPEARE

CHARACTER

The Inner Man

Beauty depends on simplicity—I mean the true simplicity
of a rightly and nobly ordered mind and character.
He is a fool who seriously inclines to weigh the beautiful by
any other standard than that of the good.
The good is the beautiful.
Grant me to be beautiful in the inner man.

PLATO

The Noble Nature

It is not growing like a tree
　　In bulk, doth make man better be;
Or standing long an oak, three hundred year,
To fall a log at last, dry, bald, and sear:
　　A lily of a day
　　Is fairer far in May,
Although it fall and die that night,—
It was the plant and flower of Light.
In small proportions we just beauties see,
And in short measures life may perfect be.

BEN JONSON

My Mind to Me a Kingdom Is

My mind to me a kingdom is;
   Such present joys therein I find
That it excels all other bliss
   That earth affords or grows by kind.
Though much I want which most would have,
Yet still my mind forbids to crave.

No princely pomp, no wealthy store,
   No force to win the victory,
No wily wit to salve a sore,
   No shape to feed a loving eye;
To none of these I yield as thrall—
For why? My mind doth serve for all.

I see how plenty surfeits oft,
   And hasty climbers soon do fall;
I see that those which are aloft
   Mishap doth threaten most of all;
They get with toil, they keep with fear—
Such cares my mind could never bear.

Content to live, this is my stay;
  I seek no more than may suffice;
I press to bear no haughty sway;
  Look, what I lack my mind supplies.
Lo, thus I triumph like a king,
Content with that my mind doth bring.

Some have too much, yet still do crave;
  I little have, and seek no more.
They are but poor, though much they have,
  And I am rich with little store.
They poor, I rich; they beg, I give;
They lack, I leave; they pine, I live.

I laugh not at another's loss;
  I grudge not at another's pain;
No worldly waves my mind can toss;
  My state at one doth still remain.
I fear no foe, I fawn no friend;
I loathe not life, nor dread my end.

Some weigh their pleasure by their lust,
  Their wisdom by their rage of will;
Their treasure is their only trust;
  A cloakèd craft their store of skill.
But all the pleasure that I find
Is to maintain a quiet mind.

My wealth is health and perfect ease;
    My conscience clear my chief defense;
I neither seek by bribes to please,
    Nor by deceit to breed offense.
Thus do I live; thus will I die;
Would all did so as well as I!

SIR EDWARD DYER

In Men Whom Men Condemn As Ill

In men whom men condemn as ill
I find so much of goodness still,
In men whom men pronounce divine
I find so much of sin and blot,
I do not dare to draw a line
Between the two, where God has not.

JOAQUIN MILLER

We Will Speak Out

We will speak out, we will be heard,
  Though all earth's systems crack;
We will not bate a single word,
  Nor take a letter back.
Let liars fear, let cowards shrink,
  Let traitors turn away;
Whatever we have dared to think
  That dare we also say.
We speak the truth, and what care we
  For hissing and for scorn,
While some faint gleamings we can see
  Of Freedom's coming morn?

JAMES RUSSELL LOWELL

We Never Know How High We Are

We never know how high we are
Till we are asked to rise
And then if we are true to plan
Our statures touch the skies—

The Heroism we recite
Would be a normal thing
Did not ourselves the Cubits warp
For fear to be a King—

EMILY DICKINSON

A Psalm of Life

Tell me not, in mournful numbers,
  Life is but an empty dream!—
For the soul is dead that slumbers,
  And things are not what they seem.

Life is real! Life is earnest!
  And the grave is not its goal;
Dust thou art, to dust returnest,
  Was not spoken of the soul.

Not enjoyment, and not sorrow,
  Is our destined end or way;
But to act, that each to-morrow
  Finds us farther than to-day.

Art is long, and Time is fleeting,
  And our hearts, though stout and brave,
Still, like muffled drums, are beating
  Funeral marches to the grave.

In the world's broad field of battle,
  In the bivouac of Life,
Be not like dumb, driven cattle!
  Be a hero in the strife!

Trust no Future, howe'er pleasant!
　Let the dead Past bury its dead!
Act,—act in the living Present!
　Heart within, and God o'erhead!

Lives of great men all remind us
　We can make our lives sublime,
And, departing, leave behind us
　Footprints on the sands of time;

Footprints, that perhaps another,
　Sailing o'er life's solemn main,
A forlorn and shipwrecked brother,
　Seeing, shall take heart again.

Let us, then, be up and doing,
　With a heart for any fate;
Still achieving, still pursuing,
　Learn to labor and to wait.

HENRY WADSWORTH LONGFELLOW

CHILDREN

Sweet and Low

Sweet and low, sweet and low,
   Wind of the western sea,
Low, low, breathe and blow,
   Wind of the western sea!
Over the rolling waters go,
Come from the dying moon, and blow,
   Blow him again to me;
While my little one, while my pretty one, sleeps.

Sleep and rest, sleep and rest,
   Father will come to thee soon;
Rest, rest, on mother's breast,
   Father will come to thee soon;
Father will come to his babe in the nest,
Silver sails all out of the west
   Under the silver moon:
Sleep, my little one, sleep, my pretty one, sleep.

ALFRED, LORD TENNYSON

In Reference to Her Children

I had eight birds hatched in one nest,
Four cocks there were, and hens the rest.
I nursed them up with pain and care,
Nor cost, nor labour did I spare,
Till at the last they felt their wing,
Mounted the trees, and learned to sing;
Chief of the brood then took his flight
To regions far and left me quite.
My mournful chirps I after send,
Till he return, or I do end:
Leave not thy nest, thy dam and sire,
Fly back and sing amidst this choir.
My second bird did take her flight,
And with her mate flew out of sight;
Southward they both their course did bend,
And seasons twain they there did spend,
Till after blown by southern gales,
They norward steered with filled sails.
A prettier bird was no where seen,
Along the beach among the treen.
I have a third of colour white,
On whom I placed no small delight;
Coupled with mate loving and true,
Hath also bid her dam adieu;
And where Aurora first appears,

She now hath perched to spend her years.
One to the academy flew
To chat among that learned crew;
Ambition moves still in his breast
That he might chant above the rest,
Striving for more than to do well,
That nightingales he might excel.
My fifth, whose down is yet scarce gone,
Is 'mongst the shrubs and bushes flown,
And as his wings increase in strength,
On higher boughs he'll perch at length.
My other three still with me nest,
Until they're grown, then as the rest,
Or here or there they'll take their flight,
As is ordained, so shall they light.
If birds could weep, then would my tears
Let others know what are my fears
Lest this my brood some harm should catch,
And be surprised for want of watch,
Whilst pecking corn and void of care,
They fall un'wares in fowler's snare,
Or whilst on trees they sit and sing,
Some untoward boy at them do fling,
Or whilst allured with bell and glass,
The net be spread, and caught, alas.
Or lest by lime-twigs they be foiled,
Or by some greedy hawks be spoiled.
O would my young, ye saw my breast,
And knew what thoughts there sadly rest,

Great was my pain when I you bred,
Great was my care when I you fed,
Long did I keep you soft and warm,
And with my wings kept off all harm,
My cares are more and fears than ever,
My throbs such now as 'fore were never.
Alas, my birds, you wisdom want,
Of perils you are ignorant;
Oft times in grass, on trees, in flight,
Sore accidents on you may light.
O to your safety have an eye,
So happy may you live and die.
Meanwhile my days in tunes I'll spend,
Till my weak lays with me shall end.
In shady woods I'll sit and sing,
And things that past to mind I'll bring.
Once young and pleasant, as are you,
But former toys (no joys) adieu.
My age I will not once lament,
But sing, my time so near is spent.
And from the top bough take my flight
Into a country beyond sight,
Where old ones instantly grow young,
And there with seraphims set song;
No seasons cold, nor storms they see;
But spring lasts to eternity.
When each of you shall in your nest
Among your young ones take your rest,
In chirping language, oft them tell,

You had a dam that loved you well,
That did what could be done for young,
And nursed you up till you were strong,
And 'fore she once would let you fly,
She showed you joy and misery;
Taught what was good, and what was ill,
What would save life, and what would kill.
Thus gone, amongst you I may live,
And dead, yet speak, and counsel give:
Farewell, my birds, farewell adieu,
I happy am, if well with you.

ANNE BRADSTREET

The Toys

My little son, who looked from thoughtful eyes
And moved and spoke in quiet grown-up wise,
Having my law the seventh time disobeyed,
I struck him, and dismissed
With hard words and unkissed,
—His mother, who was patient, being dead.
Then, fearing lest his grief should hinder sleep,
I visited his bed,
But found him slumbering deep,
With darkened eyelids, and their lashes yet
From his late sobbing wet.
And I, with moan,
Kissing away his tears, left others of my own;
For, on a table drawn beside his head,
He had put, within his reach,
A box of counters and a red-veined stone,
A piece of glass abraded by the beach,
And six or seven shells,
A bottle with bluebells,
And two French copper coins, ranged there with careful art,
To comfort his sad heart.
So when that night I prayed
To God, I wept, and said:

"Ah, when at last we lie with trancéd breath,
Not vexing Thee in death,
And Thou rememberest of what toys
We made our joys,
How weakly understood
Thy great commanded good,
Then, fatherly not less
Than I whom Thou hast molded from the clay,
Thou'lt leave Thy wrath, and say,
'I will be sorry for their childishness.'"

COVENTRY PATMORE

Among School Children

I walk through the long schoolroom questioning;
A kind old nun in a white hood replies;
The children learn to cipher and to sing,
To study reading-books and history,
To cut and sew, be neat in everything
In the best modern way—the children's eyes
In momentary wonder stare upon
A sixty-year-old smiling public man.

I dream of a Ledaean body, bent
Above a sinking fire, a tale that she
Told of a harsh reproof, or trivial event
That changed some childish day to tragedy—
Told, and it seemed that our two natures blent
Into a sphere from youthful sympathy,
Or else, to alter Plato's parable,
Into the yolk and the white of one shell.

III

And thinking of that fit of grief or rage
I look upon one child or t'other there
And wonder if she stood so at that age—
For even daughters of the swan can share
Something of every paddler's heritage—
And had that color upon cheek or hair,
And thereupon my heart is driven wild:
She stands before me as a living child.

IV

Her present image floats into the mind—
Did Quattrocento finger fashion it
Hollow of cheek as though it drank the wind
And took a mess of shadows for its meat?
And I though never of Ledaean kind
Had pretty plumage once—enough of that,
Better to smile on all that smile, and show
There is a comfortable kind of scarecrow.

V

What youthful mother, a shape upon her lap
Honey of generation had betrayed,
And that must sleep, shriek, struggle to escape
As recollection or the drug decide,
Would think her son, did she but see that shape
With sixty or more winters on its head,
A compensation for the pang of his birth,
Or the uncertainty of his setting forth?

VI

Plato thought nature but a spume that plays
Upon a ghostly paradigm of things;
Solider Aristotle played the taws
Upon the bottom of a king of kings;
World-famous golden-thighed Pythagoras
Fingered upon a fiddle-stick or strings
What a star sang and careless Muses heard:
Old clothes upon old sticks to scare a bird.

VII

Both nuns and mothers worship images,
But those the candles light are not as those
That animate a mother's reveries,
But keep a marble or a bronze repose.
And yet they too break hearts—O Presences
That passion, piety or affection knows,
And that all heavenly glory symbolize—
O self-born mockers of man's enterprise;

VIII

Labor is blossoming or dancing where
The body is not bruised to pleasure soul,
Nor beauty born out of its own despair,
Nor blear-eyed wisdom out of midnight oil.
O chestnut tree, great rooted blossomer,
Are you the leaf, the blossom or the bole?
O body swayed to music, O brightening glance,
How can we know the dancer from the dance?

WILLIAM BUTLER YEATS

There Was a Child Went Forth

There was a child went forth every day,
And the first object he look'd upon, that object he became,
And that object became part of him for the day or a certain
   part of the day,
Or for many years or stretching cycles of years.

The early lilacs became part of this child,
And grass and white and red morning-glories, and white
   and red clover, and the song of the phœbe-bird,
And the Third-month lambs and the sow's pink-faint litter,
   and the mare's foal and the cow's calf,
And the noisy brood of the barnyard or by the mire of the
   pond-side,
And the fish suspending themselves so curiously below
   there, and the beautiful curious liquid,
And the water-plants with their graceful flat heads, all
   became part of him.

The field-sprouts of Fourth-month and Fifth-month became part of him,
Winter-grain sprouts and those of the light-yellow corn, and the esculent roots of the garden,
And the apple-trees cover'd with blossoms and the fruit afterward, and wood-berries, and the commonest weeds by the road,
And the old drunkard staggering home from the outhouse of the tavern whence he had lately risen,
And the schoolmistress that pass'd on her way to the school,
And the friendly boys that pass'd, and the quarrelsome boys,
And the tidy and fresh-cheek'd girls, and the barefoot negro boy and girl,
And all the changes of city and country wherever he went.

His own parents, he that had father'd him and she that had conceiv'd him in her womb and birth'd him,
They gave this child more of themselves than that,
They gave him afterward every day, they became part of him.

The mother at home quietly placing the dishes on the supper-table,

The mother with mild words, clean her cap and gown, a wholesome odor falling off her person and clothes as she walks by.

The father, strong, self-sufficient, manly, mean, anger'd, unjust,

The blow, the quick loud word, the tight bargain, the crafty lure,

The family usages, the language, the company, the furniture, the yearning and swelling heart,

Affection that will not be gainsay'd, the sense of what is real, the thought if after all it should prove unreal,

The doubts of day-time and the doubts of night-time, the curious whether and how,

Whether that which appears so is so, or is it all flashes and specks?

Men and women crowding fast in the streets, if they are not flashes and specks what are they?

The streets themselves and the façades of houses, and goods in the windows,

Vehicles, teams, the heavy-plank'd wharves, the huge crossing at the ferries,

The village on the highland seen from afar at sunset, the river between,

Shadows, aureola and mist, the light falling on roofs and gables of white or brown two miles off,

The schooner near by sleepily dropping down the tide, the little boat slack-tow'd astern,

The hurrying tumbling waves, quick-broken crests, slap-
   ing,
The strata of color'd clouds, the long bar of maroon-tint
   away solitary by itself, the spread of purity it lies motion-
   less in,
The horizon's edge, the flying sea-crow, the fragrance of
   salt marsh and shore mud,
These became part of that child who went forth every day,
   and who now goes, and will always go forth every day.

WALT WHITMAN

CAMARADERIE

from *Devotions XVII*

No man is an island, entire of itself;
every man is a piece of the continent,
   a part of the main;
. . . any man's death diminishes me, because
   I am involved in mankind;
and therefore never send to know for whom the bell tolls;
it tolls for thee.

JOHN DONNE

I'm Nobody! Who Are You?

I'm Nobody! Who are you?
Are you—Nobody—Too?
Then there's a pair of us?
Don't tell! they'd advertise—you know!

How dreary—to be—Somebody!
How public—like a Frog—
To tell one's name—the livelong June—
To an admiring Bog!

EMILY DICKINSON

Friendship Is Love Without His Wings

Why should my anxious breast repine,
  Because my youth is fled?
Days of delight may still be mine;
  Affection is not dead.
In tracing back the years of youth,
One firm record, one lasting truth
  Celestial consolation brings;
Bear it, ye breezes, to the seat
Where first my heart responsive beat,—
  "Friendship is Love without his wings!"

GEORGE GORDON, LORD BYRON

I Died for Beauty

I died for beauty—but was scarce
Adjusted in the tomb
When One who died for Truth, was lain
In an adjoining Room—

He questioned softly "Why I failed"?
"For Beauty," I replied—
"And I—for Truth—Themself are One—
We Brethren, are," He said—

And so, as Kinsmen met a Night—
We talked between the Rooms—
Until the Moss had reached our lips—
And covered up—our names—

EMILY DICKINSON

CONSEQUENCES

The Road Not Taken

Two roads diverged in a yellow wood,
And sorry I could not travel both
And be one traveler, long I stood
And looked down one as far as I could
To where it bent in the undergrowth;

Then took the other, as just as fair,
And having perhaps the better claim,
Because it was grassy and wanted wear;
Though as for that the passing there
Had worn them really about the same,

And both that morning equally lay
In leaves no step had trodden black.
Oh, I kept the first for another day!
Yet knowing how way leads on to way,
I doubted if I should ever come back.

I shall be telling this with a sigh
Somewhere ages and ages hence:
Two roads diverged in a wood, and I—
I took the one less traveled by,
And that has made all the difference.

ROBERT FROST

You Never Can Tell

You never can tell when you send a word
    Like an arrow shot from a bow
By an archer blind, be it cruel or kind,
    Just where it may chance to go.
It may pierce the breast of your dearest friend,
    Tipped with its poison or balm,
To a stranger's heart in life's great mart
    It may carry its pain or its calm.

ELLA WHEELER WILCOX

CREED

Count That Day Lost

If you sit down at set of sun
And count the acts that you have done,
  And, counting, find
One self-denying deed, one word
That eased the heart of him who heard,
  One glance most kind
That fell like sunshine where it went—
Then you may count that day well spent.

But if, through all the livelong day,
You've cheered no heart, by yea or nay—
  If, through it all
You've nothing done that you can trace
That brought the sunshine to one face—
  No act most small
That helped some soul and nothing cost—
Then count that day as worse than lost.

GEORGE ELIOT

For This Is Wisdom

For this is Wisdom; to love, to live,
To take what Fate, or the Gods, may give,
To ask no question, to make no prayer,
To kiss the lips and caress the hair,
Speed passion's ebb as you greet its flow,—
To have,—to hold,—and,—in time,—let go!

LAURENCE HOPE

Perseverance

If a task is once begun
Never leave it till it's done.
Be the labor great or small,
Do it well or not at all.

ANONYMOUS

John Wesley's Rule

Do all the good you can,
By all the means you can,
In all the ways you can,
In all the places you can,
At all the times you can,
To all the people you can,
As long as ever you can.

With Every Rising of the Sun

With every rising of the sun
Think of your life as just begun.

The past has shrived and buried deep
All yesterdays—there let them sleep. . . .

Concern yourself with but today,
Woo it and teach it to obey,

Your wish and will. Since time began
Today has been the friend of man. . . .

You and today! a soul sublime
And the great pregnant hour of time.

With God between to bind the twain—
Go forth I say—attain—attain.

ELLA WHEELER WILCOX

DISILLUSIONMENT

Pity Me Not

Pity me not because the light of day
At close of day no longer walks the sky;
Pity me not for beauties passed away
From field and thicket as the year goes by;
Pity me not the waning of the moon,
Nor that the ebbing tide goes out to sea,
Nor that a man's desire is hushed so soon,
And you no longer look with love on me.
This have I known always: Love is no more
Than the wide blossom which the wind assails,
Than the great tide that treads the shifting shore,
Strewing fresh wreckage gathered in the gales;
Pity me that the heart is slow to learn
What the swift mind beholds at every turn.

EDNA ST. VINCENT MILLAY

70

The Hollow Men

Mistah Kurtz—he dead.

                      A penny for the Old Guy.

I

We are the hollow men
We are the stuffed men
Leaning together
Headpiece filled with straw. Alas!
Our dried voices, when
We whisper together
Are quiet and meaningless
As wind in dry grass
Or rats' feet over broken glass
In our dry cellar

Shape without form, shade without color,
Paralyzed force, gesture without motion:
Those who have crossed
With direct eyes, to death's other Kingdom
Remember us—if at all—not as lost
Violent souls, but only
As the hollow men
The stuffed men.

II

Eyes I dare not meet in dreams
In death's dream kingdom
These do not appear:
There, the eyes are
Sunlight on a broken column
There, is a tree swinging
And voices are
In the wind's singing
More distant and more solemn
Than a fading star.

Let me be no nearer
In death's dream kingdom
Let me also wear
Such deliberate disguises
Rat's coat, crowskin, crossed staves
In a field
Behaving as the wind behaves
No nearer—

Not that final meeting
In the twilight kingdom

III

This is the dead land
This is cactus land
Here the stone images
Are raised, here they receive
The supplication of a dead man's hand
Under the twinkle of a fading star.

Is it like this
In death's other kingdom
Waking alone
At the hour when we are
Trembling with tenderness
Lips that would kiss
Form prayers to broken stone.

IV

The eyes are not here
There are no eyes here
In this valley of dying stars
In this hollow valley
This broken jaw of our lost kingdoms

In this last of meeting places
We grope together
And avoid speech
Gathered on this beach of the tumid river

Sightless, unless
The eyes reappear
As the perpetual star
Multifoliate rose
Of death's twilight kingdom
The hope only
Of empty men.

V

Here we go round the prickly pear
Prickly pear prickly pear
Here we go round the prickly pear
At five o'clock in the morning.

Between the idea
And the reality
Between the motion
And the act
Falls the Shadow

For Thine is the Kingdom

Between the conception
And the creation
Between the emotion
And the response
Falls the Shadow

      Life is very long

Between the desire
And the spasm
Between the potency
And the existence
Between the essence
And the descent
Falls the Shadow

     For Thine is the Kingdom

For Thine is
Life is
For Thine is the

This is the way the world ends
This is the way the world ends
This is the way the world ends
Not with a bang but a whimper.

       T. S. ELIOT

ELEGY

The Martyr

Indicative of the passion of the people on the 15th of April 1865

Good Friday was the day
  Of the prodigy and crime,
When they killed him in his pity,
  When they killed him in his prime
Of clemency and calm—
    When with yearning he was filled
    To redeem the evil-willed,
And, though conqueror, be kind;
  But they killed him in his kindness,
  In their madness and their blindness,
And they killed him from behind.

There is sobbing of the strong,
  And a pall upon the land;
But the People in their weeping
      Bare the iron hand:
Beware the People weeping
  When they bare the iron hand.

He lieth in his blood—
  The father in his face;
They have killed him, the Forgiver—
  The Avenger takes his place,
The Avenger wisely stern,
    Who in righteousness shall do
    What the heavens call him to,
And the parricides remand;
  For they killed him in his kindness,
  In their madness and their blindness,
And his blood is on their hand.

There is sobbing of the strong,
  And a pall upon the land;
But the People in their weeping
      Bare the iron hand:
Beware the People weeping
  When they bare the iron hand.

HERMAN MELVILLE

To an Athlete Dying Young

The time you won your town the race
We chaired you through the market-place;
Man and boy stood cheering by,
And home we brought you shoulder-high.

Today, the road all runners come,
Shoulder-high we bring you home,
And set you at your threshold down,
Townsman of a stiller town.

Smart lad, to slip betimes away
From fields where glory does not stay,
And early though the laurel grows
It withers quicker than the rose.

Eyes the shady night has shut
Cannot see the record cut,
And silence sounds no worse than cheers
After death has stopped the ears:

Now you will not swell the rout
Of lads that wore their honors out,
Runners whom renown outran
And the name died before the man.

So set, before its echoes fade,
The fleet foot on the sill of shade,
And hold to the low lintel up
The still-defended challenge-cup.

And round that early-laureled head
Will flock to gaze the strengthless dead,
And find unwithered on its curls
The garland briefer than a girl's.

A. E. HOUSMAN

When Lilacs Last in the Dooryard Bloomed

1

When lilacs last in the dooryard bloomed,
And the great star early drooped in the western sky in the
  night,
I mourned, and yet shall mourn with ever-returning spring.

Ever-returning spring, trinity sure to me you bring,
Lilac blooming perennial and drooping star in the west,
And thought of him I love.

2

O powerful western fallen star!
O shades of night—O moody, tearful night!
O great star disappeared—O the black murk that hides the
  star!
O cruel hands that hold me powerless—O helpless soul of
  me!
O harsh surrounding cloud that will not free my soul.

3

In the dooryard fronting an old farmhouse near the white-
     washed palings,
Stands the lilac bush tall-growing with heart-shaped leaves
     of rich green,
With many a pointed blossom rising delicate, with the per-
     fume strong I love,
With every leaf a miracle—and from this bush in the door-
     yard,
With delicate-colored blossoms and heart-shaped leaves of
     rich green,
A sprig with its flower I break.

In the swamp in secluded recesses,
A shy and hidden bird is warbling a song.

Solitary the thrush,
The hermit withdrawn to himself, avoiding the settle-
     ments,
Sings by himself a song.

Song of the bleeding throat,
Death's outlet song of life (for well dear brother I know,
If thou wast not granted to sing thou wouldst surely die).

Over the breast of the spring, the land, amid cities,
Amid lanes and through old woods, where lately the violets
   peeped from the ground, spotting the gray debris,
Amid the grass in the fields each side of the lanes, passing
   the endless grass,
Passing the yellow-speared wheat, every grain from its
   shroud in the dark-brown fields uprisen,
Passing the apple-tree blows of white and pink in the
   orchards,
Carrying a corpse to where it shall rest in the grave,
Night and day journeys a coffin.

6

Coffin that passes through lanes and streets,
Through day and night with the great cloud darkening the
   land,
With the pomp of the inlooped flags with the cities draped
   in black,
With the show of the States themselves as of crape-veiled
   women standing,
With processions long and winding and the flambeaus of
   the night,
With the countless torches lit, with the silent sea of faces
   and the unbared heads,
With the waiting depot, the arriving coffin, and the somber
   faces,

With dirges through the night, with the thousand voices
  rising strong and solemn,
With all the mournful voices of the dirges poured around
  the coffin,
The dim-lit churches and the shuddering organs—where
  amid these you journey,
With the tolling tolling bells' perpetual clang,
Here, coffin that slowly passes,
I give you my sprig of lilac.

7

(Nor for you, for one alone,
Blossoms and branches green to coffins all I bring,
For fresh as the morning, thus would I chant a song for you
  O sane and sacred death,
All over bouquets of roses,
O death, I cover you over with roses and early lilies,
But mostly and now the lilac that blooms the first,
Copious I break, I break the sprigs from the bushes,
With loaded arms I come, pouring for you,
For you and the coffins all of you O death.)

8

O western orb sailing the heaven,
Now I know what you must have meant as a month since I
  walked,
As I walked in silence the transparent shadowy night,

As I saw you had something to tell as you bent to me night
after night,

As you drooped from the sky low down as if to my side
(while the other stars all looked on),

As we wandered together the solemn night (for something
I know not what kept me from sleep),

As the night advanced, and I saw on the rim of the west
how full you were of woe,

As I stood on the rising ground in the breeze in the cool
transparent night,

As I watched where you passed and was lost in the nether-
ward black of the night,

As my soul in its trouble dissatisfied sank, as where you sad
orb,

Concluded, dropped in the night, and was gone.

9

Sing on there in the swamp,

O singer bashful and tender, I hear your notes, I hear your
call,

I hear, I come presently, I understand you,

But a moment I linger, for the lustrous star has detained
me,

The star my departing comrade holds and detains me.

10

O how shall I warble myself for the dead one there I loved?

And how shall I deck my song for the large sweet soul that
has gone?

And what shall my perfume be for the grave of him I love?

Sea winds blown from east and west,

Blown from the Eastern sea and blown from the Western
sea, till there on the prairies meeting,

These and with these and the breath of my chant,

I'll perfume the grave of him I love.

11

O what shall I hang on the chamber walls?

And what shall the pictures be that I hang on the walls,

To adorn the burial house of him I love?

Pictures of growing spring and farms and homes,

With the Fourth-month eve at sundown, and the gray
smoke lucid and bright,

With floods of the yellow gold of the gorgeous, indolent,
sinking sun, burning, expanding the air

With the fresh sweet herbage underfoot, and the pale green
leaves of the trees prolific,

In the distance the flowing glaze, the breast of the river,
with a wind dapple here and there,

With ranging hills on the banks, with many a line against
the sky, and shadows,

And the city at hand with dwellings so dense, and stacks of
   chimneys,
And all the scenes of life and the workshops, and the work-
   men homeward returning.

12

Lo, body and soul—this land,
My own Manhattan with spires, and the sparkling and
   hurrying tides, and the ships,
The varied and ample land, the South and the North in the
   light, Ohio's shores and flashing Missouri,
And ever the far-spreading prairies covered with grass and
   corn.
Lo, the most excellent sun so calm and haughty,
The violet and purple morn with just-felt breezes,
The gentle soft-born measureless light,
The miracle spreading bathing all, the fulfilled moon,
The coming eve delicious, the welcome night and the stars,
Over my cities shining all, enveloping man and land.

13

Sing on, sing on you gray-brown bird,
Sing from the swamps, the recesses, pour your chant from
   the bushes,
Limitless out of the dusk, out of the cedars and pines.
Sing on dearest brother, warble your reedy song,
Loud human song, with voice of uttermost woe.

O liquid and free and tender!
O wild and loose to my soul—O wondrous singer!
You only I hear—yet the star holds me (but will soon de-
    part),
Yet the lilac with mastering odor holds me.

14

Now while I sat in the day and looked forth,
In the close of the day with its light and the fields of spring,
    and the farmers preparing their crops,
In the large unconscious scenery of my land with its lakes
    and forests,
In the heavenly aerial beauty (after the perturbed winds
    and the storms),
Under the arching heavens of the afternoon swift passing,
    and the voices of children and women,
The many-moving sea tides, and I saw the ships how they
    sailed,
And the summer approaching with richness, and the fields
    all busy with labor,
And the infinite separate houses, how they all went on,
    each with its meals and minutia of daily usages,
And the streets how their throbbings throbbed, and the
    cities pent—lo, then and there,
Falling upon them all and among them all, enveloping me
    with the rest,
Appeared the cloud, appeared the long black trail,

And I knew death, its thought, and the sacred knowledge of
   death.

Then with the knowledge of death as walking one side of
   me,
And the thought of death close-walking the other side of
   me,
And I in the middle as with companions, and as holding the
   hands of companions,
I fled forth to the hiding receiving night that talks not,
Down to the shores of the water the path by the swamp in
   the dimness,
To the solemn shadowy cedars and ghostly pines so still,
And the singer so shy to the rest received me,
The gray-brown bird I know received us comrades three,
And he sang the carol of death, and a verse for him I love.
From deep secluded recesses
From the fragrant cedars and the ghostly pines so still,
Came the carol of the bird.
And the charm of the carol rapt me,
As I held as if by their hands my comrades in the night,
And the voice of my spirit tallied the song of the bird.

Come lovely and soothing death,
Undulate round the world, serenely arriving, arriving,
In the day, in the night, to all, to each,
Sooner or later delicate death.
Praised be the fathomless universe,

For life and joy, and for objects and knowledge curious,
And for love, sweet love—but praise! praise! praise!
For the sure-enwinding arms of cool-enfolding death.
Dark mother always gliding near with soft feet,
Have none chanted for thee a chant of fullest welcome?
Then I chant it for thee, I glorify thee above all,
I bring thee a song that when thou must indeed come, come unfalteringly.
Approach strong deliveress,
When it is so, when thou hast taken them I joyously sing the dead,
Lost in the loving floating ocean of thee,
Laved in the flood of thy bliss O death.
From me to thee glad serenades,
Dances for thee I propose saluting thee, adornments and feastings for
    thee,
And the sights of the open landscape and the high-spread sky are fitting,
And life and the fields, and the huge and thoughtful night.
The night in silence under many a star,
The ocean shore and the husky whispering wave whose voice I know,
And the soul turning to thee O vast and well-veiled death,
And the body gratefully nestling close to thee.
Over the treetops I float thee a song,
Over the rising and sinking waves, over the myriad fields and the
    prairies wide,
Over the dense-packed cities all and the teeming wharves and ways,
I float this carol with joy, with joy to thee O death.

To the tally of my soul,
Loud and strong kept up the gray-brown bird,
With pure deliberate notes spreading filling the night.
Loud in the pines and cedars dim,
Clear in the freshness moist and the swamp perfume,
And I with my comrades there in the night.
While my sight that was bound in my eyes unclosed,
As to long panoramas of visions.
And I saw askant the armies,
I saw as in noiseless dreams hundreds of battle flags,
Borne through the smoke of the battles and pierced with
    missiles I saw them,
And carried hither and yon through the smoke, and torn
    and bloody,
And at last but a few shreds left on the staffs (and all in
    silence),
And the staffs all splintered and broken.
I saw battle corpses, myriads of them,
And the white skeletons of young men, I saw them,
I saw the debris and debris of all the slain soldiers of the
    war,
But I saw they were not as was thought,
They themselves were fully at rest, they suffered not,
The living remained and suffered, the mother suffered,
And the wife and the child and the musing comrade suf-
    fered,
And the armies that remained suffered.

Passing the visions, passing the night,

Passing, unloosing the hold of my comrades' hands,

Passing the song of the hermit bird and the tallying song of
my soul,

Victorious song, death's outlet song, yet varying ever-alter-
ing song,

As low and wailing, yet clear the notes, rising and falling,
flooding the night,

Sadly sinking and fainting, as warning and warning, and yet
again bursting with joy,

Covering the earth and filling the spread of the heaven,

As that powerful psalm in the night I heard from recesses,

Passing, I leave thee lilac with heart-shaped leaves,

I leave thee there in the dooryard, blooming, returning with
spring.

I cease from my song for thee,

From my gaze on thee in the west, fronting the west,
communing with thee,

O comrade lustrous with silver face in the night.

Yet each to keep and all, retrievements out of the night,
The song, the wondrous chant of the gray-brown bird,
And the tallying chant, the echo aroused in my soul,
With the lustrous and drooping star with the countenance
full of woe,
With the holders holding my hand nearing the call of the
bird,
Comrades mine and I in the midst, and their memory ever
to keep, for the dead I loved so well,
For the sweetest, wisest soul of all my days and lands—and
this for his dear sake,
Lilac and star and bird twined with the chant of my soul,
There in the fragrant pines and the cedars dusk and dim.

WALT WHITMAN

ETERNITY

Song's Eternity

What is song's eternity?
   Come and see.
Can it noise and bustle be?
   Come and see.

Praises sung or praises said
   Can it be?
Wait awhile and these are dead—
   Sigh, sigh;
Be they high or lowly bred
   They die.

What is song's eternity?
   Come and see.
Melodies of earth and sky,
   Here they be.

Song once sung to Adam's ears
    Can it be?
Ballads of six thousand years
    Thrive, thrive;
Songs awaken with the spheres
    Alive.

Mighty songs that miss decay,
    What are they?
Crowds and cities pass away
    Like a day.

Books are out and books are read;
    What are they?
Years will lay them with the dead—
    Sigh, sigh;
Trifles unto nothing wed,
    They die.

Dreamers, mark the honey bee;
    Mark the tree
Where the blue cap "tootle tee"
    Sings a glee

Sung to Adam and to Eve—
   Here they be.
When floods covered every bough,
   Noah's ark
Heard that ballad singing now;
   Hark, hark,

"Tootle tootle tootle tee"—
   Can it be
Pride and fame must shadows be?
   Come and see—

Every season owns her own;
   Bird and bee
Sing creation's music on;
   Nature's glee
Is in every mood and tone
   Eternity.

                    JOHN CLARE

And Death Shall Have No Dominion

And death shall have no dominion.
Dead men naked they shall be one
With the man in the wind and the west moon;
When their bones are picked clean and the clean bones
   gone,
They shall have stars at elbow and foot;
Though they go mad they shall be sane,
Though they sink through the sea they shall rise again;
Though lovers be lost love shall not;
And death shall have no dominion.

And death shall have no dominion.
Under the windings of the sea
They lying long shall not die windily;
Twisting on racks when sinews give way,
Strapped to a wheel, yet they shall not break;
Faith in their hands shall snap in two,
And the unicorn evils run them through;
Split all ends up they shan't crack;
And death shall have no dominion.

And death shall have no dominion.
No more may gulls cry at their ears
Or waves break loud on the seashores;
Where blew a flower may a flower no more
Lift its head to the blows of the rain;
Though they be mad and dead as nails,
Heads of the characters hammer through daisies;
Break in the sun till the sun breaks down,
And death shall have no dominion.

DYLAN THOMAS

FACING
DEATH

Dirge in Woods

A wind sways the pines,
        And below
Not a breath of wild air;
Still as the mosses that glow
On the flooring and over the lines
Of the roots here and there.
The pine tree drops its dead;
They are quiet, as under the sea.
Overhead, overhead
Rushes life in a race,
As the clouds the clouds chase;
        And we go,
And we drop like the fruits of the tree,
        Even we,
        Even so.

GEORGE MEREDITH

When I Have Fears

When I have fears that I may cease to be
Before my pen has glean'd my teeming brain,
Before high-piled books, in charact'ry
Hold like rich garners the full-ripen'd grain;

When I behold, upon the night's starr'd face,
Huge cloudy symbols of a high romance,
And think that I may never live to trace
Their shadows, with the magic hand of chance

And when I feel, fair Creature of an hour!
That I shall never look upon thee more,
Never have relish in the faery power
Of unreflecting love—then on the shore

Of the wide world I stand alone, and think
Till Love and Fame to nothingness do sink.

JOHN KEATS

A Slumber Did My Spirit Seal

A slumber did my spirit seal;
　I had no human fears:
She seemed a thing that could not feel
　The touch of earthly years.

No motion has she now, no force;
　She neither hears nor sees;
Rolled round in earth's diurnal course,
　With rocks, and stones, and trees.

WILLIAM WORDSWORTH

I Heard a Fly Buzz When I Died

I heard a Fly buzz—when I died—
The Stillness in the Room
Was like the Stillness in the Air—
Between the Heaves of Storm—

The Eyes around—had wrung them dry—
And Breaths were gathering firm
For that last Onset—when the King
Be witnessed—in the Room—

I willed my Keepsakes—Signed away
What portions of me be
Assignable—and then it was
There interposed a Fly—

With Blue—uncertain stumbling Buzz—
Between the light—and me—
And then the Windows failed—and then
I could not see to see—

EMILY DICKINSON

A Parting Guest

What delightful hosts are they—
    Life and Love!
Lingeringly I turn away,
    This late hour, yet glad enough
They have not withheld from me
    Their high hospitality.
So, with face lit with delight
    And all gratitude, I stay
    Yet to press their hands and say,
"Thanks,—So fine a time! Good night."

JAMES WHITCOMB RILEY

Nature

As a fond mother, when the day is o'er,
　　Leads by the hand her little child to bed,
　　Half willing, half reluctant to be led,
　　And leave his broken playthings on the floor,
Still gazing at them through the open door,
　　Nor wholly reassured and comforted
　　By promises of others in their stead,
　　Which, though more splendid, may not please him more;
So Nature deals with us, and takes away
　　Our playthings one by one, and by the hand
　　Leads us to rest so gently, that we go
Scarce knowing if we wish to go or stay,
　　Being too full of sleep to understand
　　How far the unknown transcends the what we know.

HENRY WADSWORTH LONGFELLOW

The Last Invocation

At the last, tenderly,
From the walls of the powerful fortress'd house,
From the clasp of the knitted locks, from the keep of the
   well-closed doors,
Let me be wafted.

Let me glide noiselessly forth;
With the key of softness unlock the locks—with a whisper,
Set ope the doors O soul.

Tenderly—be not impatient,
(Strong is your hold O mortal flesh.
Strong is your hold O love.)

WALT WHITMAN

Tract

I will teach you my townspeople
how to perform a funeral—
for you have it over a troop
of artists—
unless one should scour the world—
you have the ground sense necessary.

See! the hearse leads.
I begin with a design for a hearse.
For Christ's sake not black—
nor white either—and not polished!
Let it be weathered—like a farm wagon—
with gilt wheels (this could be
applied fresh at small expense)
or no wheels at all:
a rough dray to drag over the ground.

Knock the glass out!
My God—glass, my townspeople!
For what purpose? Is it for the dead
to look out or for us to see
how well he is housed or to see
the flowers or the lack of them—
or what?

To keep the rain and snow from him?
He will have a heavier rain soon:
pebbles and dirt and what not.
Let there be no glass—
and no upholstery! phew!
and no little brass rollers
and small easy wheels on the bottom—
my townspeople what are you thinking of!

A rough plain hearse then
with gilt wheels and no top at all.
On this the coffin lies
by its own weight.

              No wreaths please—
especially no hot-house flowers.
Some common memento is better,
something he prized and is known by:
his old clothes—a few books perhaps—
God knows what! You realize
how we are about these things,
my townspeople—
something will be found—anything—
even flowers if he had come to that.
So much for the hearse.

For heaven's sake though see to the driver!
Take off the silk hat! In fact
that's no place at all for him
up there unceremoniously
dragging our friend out of his own dignity!
Bring him down—bring him down!
Low and inconspicuous! I'd not have him ride
on the wagon at all—damn him—
the undertaker's understrapper!
Let him hold the reins
and walk at the side
and inconspicuously too!

Then briefly as to yourselves:
Walk behind—as they do in France,
seventh class, or if you ride
Hell take curtains! Go with some show
of inconvenience, sit openly—
to the weather as to grief.
Or do you think you can shut grief in?
What—from us? We who have perhaps
nothing to lose? Share with us
share with us—it will be money
in your pockets.

                    Go now
I think you are ready.

WILLIAM CARLOS WILLIAMS

Thanatopsis

To him who in the love of Nature holds
Communion with her visible forms, she speaks
A various language; for his gayer hours
She has a voice of gladness, and a smile
And eloquence of beauty, and she glides
Into his darker musings, with a mild
And healing sympathy that steals away
Their sharpness, ere he is aware. When thoughts
Of the last bitter hour come like a blight
Over the spirit, and sad images

Of the stern agony, and shroud, and pall,
And breathless darkness, and the narrow house,
Make thee to shudder, and grow sick at heart;—
Go forth, under the open sky, and list
To Nature's teachings, while from all around—
Earth and her waters, and the depths of air—
Comes a still voice—Yet a few days, and thee
The all-beholding sun shall see no more
In all his course; nor yet in the cold ground,
Where thy pale form was laid, with many tears,

Nor in the embrace of ocean, shall exist
Thy image. Earth, that nourished thee, shall claim
Thy growth, to be resolved to earth again,
And, lost each human trace, surrendering up
Thine individual being, shalt thou go
To mix for ever with the elements,
To be a brother to the insensible rock
And to the sluggish clod, which the rude swain
Turns with his share, and treads upon. The oak
Shall send his roots abroad, and pierce thy mould.

 Yet not to thine eternal resting-place
Shalt thou retire alone, nor couldst thou wish
Couch more magnificent. Thou shalt lie down
With patriarchs of the infant world—with kings,
The powerful of the earth—the wise, the good,
Fair forms, and hoary seers of ages past,
All in one mighty sepulchre. The hills
Rock-ribbed and ancient as the sun,—the vales
Stretching in pensive quietness between;
The venerable woods—rivers that move
In majesty, and the complaining brooks
That make the meadows green; and, poured round all,
Old Ocean's gray and melancholy waste,—
Are but the solemn decorations all
Of the great tomb of man. The golden sun,

The planets, all the infinite host of heaven,
Are shining on the sad abodes of death,
Through the still lapse of ages. All that tread
The globe are but a handful to the tribes
That slumber in its bosom.—Take the wings
Of morning, pierce the Barcan wilderness,
Or lose thyself in the continuous woods
Where rolls the Oregon, and hears no sound,
Save his own dashings—yet the dead are there:
And millions in those solitudes, since first
The flight of years began, have laid them down
In their last sleep—the dead reign there alone.
So shalt thou rest, and what if thou withdraw
In silence from the living, and no friend
Take note of thy departure? All that breathe
Will share thy destiny. The gay will laugh
When thou art gone, the solemn brood of care
Plod on, and each one as before will chase
His favorite phantom; yet all these shall leave
Their mirth and their employments, and shall come
And make their bed with thee. As the long train
Of ages glide away, the sons of men,
The youth in life's green spring, and he who goes
In the full strength of years, matron and maid,
The speechless babe, and the gray-headed man—
Shall one by one be gathered to thy side,
By those, who in their turn shall follow them.

So live, that when thy summons comes to join
The innumerable caravan, which moves
To that mysterious realm, where each shall take
His chamber in the silent halls of death,
Thou go not, like the quarry-slave at night,
Scourged to his dungeon, but, sustained and soothed
By an unfaltering trust, approach thy grave,
Like one who wraps the drapery of his couch
About him, and lies down to pleasant dreams.

WILLIAM CULLEN BRYANT

FAITH

After-Thought

I thought of Thee, my partner and my guide,
As being past away.—Vain sympathies!
For, backward, Duddon! as I cast my eyes,
I see what was, and is, and will abide;
Still glides the Stream, and shall for ever glide;
The Form remains, the Function never dies;
While we, the brave, the mighty, and the wise,
We Men, who in our morn of youth defied
The elements, must vanish;—be it so!
Enough, if something from our hands have power
To live, and act, and serve the future hour;
And if, as toward the silent tomb we go,
Through love, through hope, and faith's transcendent dower,
We feel that we are greater than we know.

WILLIAM WORDSWORTH

God

I see Thee in the distant blue;
But in the violet's dell of dew,
Behold, I *breathe and touch* Thee too.

JOHN BANISTER TABB

Surprised by Joy

Surprised by joy—impatient as the Wind
I turned to share the transport—Oh! with whom
But Thee, deep buried in the silent tomb,
That spot which no vicissitude can find?
Love, faithful love, recalled thee to my mind—
But how could I forget thee? Through what power,
Even for the least division of an hour,
Have I been so beguiled as to be blind
To my most grievous loss!—That thought's return
Was the worst pang that sorrow ever bore,
Save one, one only, when I stood forlorn,
Knowing my heart's best treasure was no more;
That neither present time, nor years unborn
Could to my sight that heavenly face restore.

WILLIAM WORDSWORTH

O Never Star Was Lost

O never star
Was lost; here
We all aspire to heaven and there is heaven
Above us.
If I stoop
Into a dark tremendous sea of cloud,
It is but for a time; I press God's lamp
Close to my breast; its splendor soon or late
Will pierce the gloom. I shall emerge some day.

ROBERT BROWNING

Chariot of Fire

And did those feet in ancient time
Walk upon England's mountains green?
And was the Holy Lamb of God
On England's pleasant pastures seen?

And did the Countenance Divine
Shine forth upon our clouded hills?
And was Jerusalem builded here
Among these dark Satanic Mills?

Bring me my Bow of burning gold;
Bring me my Arrows of desire:
Bring me my Spear: O clouds unfold!
Bring me my Chariot of fire.

I will not cease from Mental Fight,
Nor shall my Sword sleep in my hand
Till we have built Jerusalem
In England's green and pleasant Land.

WILLIAM BLAKE

Obedience

I said, "Let me walk in the fields."
    He said, "No, walk in the town."
I said, "There are no flowers there."
    He said, "No flowers, but a crown."

I said, "But the skies are black;
    There is nothing but noise and din."
And He wept as he sent me back:
    "There is more," He said; "there is sin."

I said, "But the air is thick,
    And fogs are veiling the sun."
He answered, "Yet souls are sick,
    And souls in the dark undone."

I said, "I shall miss the light,
    And friends will miss me, they say."
He answered, "Choose to-night,
    If *I* am to miss you, or they."

I pleaded for time to be given.
    He said, "Is it hard to decide?
It will not seem hard in heaven
    To have followed the steps of your Guide."

I cast one look at the fields,
    Then set my face to the town:
He said, "My child, do you yield?
    Will you leave the flowers for the crown?"

Then into His hand went mine,
    And into my heart came He;
And I walk in a light divine
    The path I had feared to see.

GEORGE MACDONALD

FAREWELL

Farewell

Farewell! if ever fondest prayer
  For other's weal availed on high,
Mine will not all be lost in air,
  But waft thy name beyond the sky.
'Twere vain to speak, to weep, to sigh:
  Oh! more than tears of blood can tell,
When wrung from guilt's expiring eye,
  Are in that word—Farewell!—Farewell!

These lips are mute, these eyes are dry;
  But in my breast and in my brain,
Awake the pangs that pass not by,
  The thought that ne'er shall sleep again.
My soul nor deigns nor dares complain,
  Though grief and passion there rebel:
I only know we loved in vain;
  I only feel—Farewell!—Farewell!

GEORGE GORDON, LORD BYRON

Farewell! Thou Art Too Dear

Farewell! thou art too dear for my possessing,
And like enough thou know'st thy estimate:
The charter of thy worth gives thee releasing;
My bonds in thee are all determinate.
For how do I hold thee but by thy granting?
And for that riches where is my deserving?
The cause of this fair gift in me is wanting,
And so my patent back again is swerving.
Thyself thou gav'st, thy own worth then not knowing,
Or me, to whom thou gav'st it, else mistaking;
So thy great gift, upon misprison growing,
Comes home again, on better judgment making.
Thus have I had thee, as a dream doth flatter
In sleep a king; but waking, no such matter.

WILLIAM SHAKESPEARE

April Love

We have walked in Love's land a little way,
  We have learnt his lesson a little while,
And shall we not part at the end of day,
  With a sigh, a smile?

A little while in the shine of the sun,
  We were twined together, joined lips, forgot
How the shadows fall when the day is done,
  And when Love is not.

We have made no vows—there will none be broke,
  Our love was free as the wind on the hill,
There was no word said we need wish unspoke,
  We have wrought no ill.

So shall we not part at the end of day,
  Who have loved and lingered a little while,
Join lips for the last time, go our way,
  With a sigh, a smile?

ERNEST DOWSON

from *Idea*

Dear, why should you command me to my rest
When now the night doth summon all to sleep?
Methinks this time becometh lovers best;
Night was ordained together friends to keep.
How happy are all other living things
Which, though the day disjoin by several flight,
The quiet evening yet together brings,
And each returns unto his love at night.
O thou, that art so courteous else to all,
Why shouldst thou, Night, abuse me only thus,
That every creature to his kind doth call
And yet 'tis thou dost only sever us.
Well could I wish it would be ever day
If when night comes you bid me go away.

MICHAEL DRAYTON

FRUSTRATION

My Love Is Like to Ice

My love is like to ice, and I to fire:
How comes it then that this her cold so great
Is not dissolved through my so hot desire,
But harder grows the more I her entreat?
Or how comes it that my exceeding heat
Is not allayed by her heart-frozen cold,
But that I burn much more in boiling sweat,
And feel my flames augmented manifold?
What more miraculous thing may be told,
That fire, which all things melts, should harden
   ice,
And ice, which is congealed with senseless cold,
Should kindle fire by wonderful device?
Such is the power of love in gentle mind,
That it can alter all the course of kind.

EDMUND SPENSER

123

Villanelle of the Poet's Road

Wine and woman and song,
   Three things garnish our way:
Yet is day over long.

Lest we do our youth wrong,
   Gather them while we may:
Wine and woman and song.

Three things render us strong,
   Vine leaves, kisses and bay:
Yet is day over long.

Unto us they belong,
   Us the bitter and gay,
Wine and woman and song.

We, as we pass along,
   Are sad that they will not stay;
Yet is day over long.

Fruits and flowers among,
   What is better than they:
Wine and woman and song?
Yet is day over long.

ERNEST DOWSON

FUN

Epigram

You beat your pate, and fancy wit will come:
Knock as you please, there's nobody at home.

ALEXANDER POPE

The Moron

See the happy moron,
He doesn't give a damn!
I wish I were a moron—
My God! Perhaps I am!

ANONYMOUS

Explanation

I hate to be a kicker,
   I always long for peace,
But the wheel that does the squeaking,
   Is the one that gets the grease.

JOSH BILLINGS

Don't Copy Cat

Don't, like the cat, try to get more out
of an experience than there is in it.
The cat, having sat upon a hot stove lid,
Will not sit upon a hot stove lid again.
Nor upon a cold stove lid.

MARK TWAIN

Don't Let That Horse

Don't let that horse
                        eat that violin

   cried Chagall's mother

                        But he
          kept right on
                  painting

And became famous

And kept on painting
                  The Horse With Violin in Mouth

And when he finally finished it
he jumped up upon the horse
                     and rode away
      waving the violin

And then with a low bow gave it
to the first naked nude he ran across

And there were no strings
                attached

LAWRENCE FERLINGHETTI

The Pessimist

Nothing to do but work,
Nothing to eat but food,
Nothing to wear but clothes
To keep one from going nude.

Nothing to breathe but air,
Quick as a flash 'tis gone;
Nowhere to fall but off,
Nowhere to stand but on.

Nothing to comb but hair
Nowhere to sleep but in bed,
Nothing to weep but tears,
Nothing to bury but dead.

Nothing to sing but songs,
Ah, well, alas! alack!
Nowhere to go but out,
Nowhere to come but back.

Nothing to see but sights,
Nothing to quench but thirst,
Nothing to have but what we've got;
Thus thro' life we are cursed.

Nothing to strike but a gait;
Everything moves that goes.
Nothing at all but common sense
Can ever withstand these woes.

BEN KING

GRIEF

My Life Closed Twice

My life closed twice before its close—
It yet remains to see
If Immortality unveil
A third event to me

So huge, so hopeless to conceive
    As these that twice befell:
Parting is all we know of heaven,
    And all we need of hell.

EMILY DICKINSON

To One in Paradise

Thou wast all that to me, love,
  For which my soul did pine—
A green isle in the sea, love,
  A fountain and a shrine,
All wreathed with fairy fruits and flowers,
  And all the flowers were mine.

Ah, dream too bright to last!
  Ah, starry Hope! that didst arise
But to be overcast!
  A voice from out the Future cries,
"On! on!"—but o'er the Past
  (Dim gulf!) my spirit hovering lies
Mute, motionless, aghast!

For, alas! alas! with me
  The light of Life is o'er!
No more—no more—no more—
  (Such language holds the solemn sea
  To the sands upon the shore)
Shall bloom the thunder-blasted tree,
  Or the stricken eagle soar!

And all my days are trances,
   And all my nightly dreams
Are where thy dark eye glances,
   And where thy footstep gleams—
In what ethereal dances,
   By what eternal streams.

EDGAR ALLAN POE

GROWING OLD

The Oak

Live thy Life,
   Young and old,
Like yon oak,
Bright in spring,
   Living gold;

Summer-rich
   Then; and then
Autumn-changed,
Soberer-hued
   Gold again.

All his leaves
   Fallen at length,
Look, he stands,
Trunk and bough,
   Naked strength.

ALFRED, LORD TENNYSON

The Old Familiar Faces

I have had playmates, I have had companions,
In my days of childhood, in my joyful school-days,
All, all are gone, the old familiar faces.

I have been laughing, I have been carousing,
Drinking late, sitting late, with my bosom cronies,
All, all are gone, the old familiar faces.

I loved a love once, fairest among women;
Closed are her doors on me, I must not see her—
All, all are gone, the old familiar faces.

I have a friend, a kinder friend has no man;
Like an ingrate, I left my friend abruptly;
Left him, to muse on the old familiar faces.

Ghost-like I paced round the haunts of my childhood.
Earth seemed a desert I was bound to traverse,
Seeking to find the old familiar faces.

Friend of my bosom, thou more than a brother,
Why wert not thou born in my father's dwelling?
So might we talk of the old familiar faces—

How some they have died, and some they have left me,
And some are taken from me; all are departed;
All, all are gone, the old familiar faces.

CHARLES LAMB

'Tis the Last Rose of Summer

'Tis the last rose of summer
   Left blooming alone;
All her lovely companions
   Are faded and gone;
No flower of her kindred,
   No rosebud, is nigh,
To reflect back her blushes,
   To give sigh for sigh.

I'll not leave thee, thou lone one,
   To pine on the stem;
Since the lovely are sleeping,
   Go sleep thou with them.
Thus kindly I scatter
   Thy leaves o'er the bed,
Where thy mates of the garden
   Lie scentless and dead.

So soon may I follow
    When friendships decay,
And from Love's shining circle
    The gems drop away!
When true hearts lie wither'd,
    And fond ones are flown,
Oh! who would inhabit
    This bleak world alone?

THOMAS MOORE

The Old Song

When all the world is young, lad,
  And all the trees are green;
And every goose a swan, lad,
  And every lass a queen;
Then hey for boot and horse, lad,
  And round the world away!
Young blood must have its course, lad,
  And every dog his day.

When all the world is old, lad,
  And all the trees are brown;
And all the sport is stale, lad,
  And all the wheels run down;
Creep home, and take your place there
  The spent and maim'd among;
God grant you find one face there
  You loved when all was young!

CHARLES KINGSLEY

When You Are Old

When you are old and gray and full of sleep,
And nodding by the fire, take down this book,
And slowly read, and dream of the soft look
Your eyes had once, and of their shadows deep;

How many loved your moments of glad grace,
And loved your beauty with love false or true;
But one man loved the pilgrim soul in you,
And loved the sorrows of your changing face.

And bending down beside the glowing bars,
Murmur, a little sadly, how love fled
And paced upon the mountains overhead
And hid his face amid a crowd of stars.

WILLIAM BUTLER YEATS

Terminus

It is time to be old,
To take in sail:—
The god of bounds,
Who sets to seas a shore,
Came to me in his fatal rounds,
And said: 'No more!
No farther shoot
Thy broad ambitious branches, and thy root,
Fancy departs: no more invent,
Contract they firmament
To compass of a tent.
There's not enough for this and that,
Make thy option which of two;
Economize the failing river,
Nor the less revere the Giver,
Leave the many and hold the few.
Timely wise accept the terms,
Soften the fall with wary foot;
A little while
Still plan and smile,
And, fault of novel germs,
Mature the unfallen fruit.
Curse, if thou wilt, thy sires,

Bad husbands of their fires,
Who, when they gave thee breath,
Failed to bequeath
The needful sinew stark as once,
The Baresark marrow to thy bones,
But left a legacy of ebbing veins,
Inconstant heat and nerveless reins,—
Amid the Muses, left thee deaf and dumb,
Amid the gladiators, halt and numb.'

    As the bird trims her to the gale,
I trim myself to the storm of time,
I man the rudder, reef the sail,
Obey the voice at eve obeyed at prime:
'Lowly faithful, banish fear,
Right onward drive unharmed;
The port well worth the cruise, is near,
And every wave is charmed.'

RALPH WALDO EMERSON

HOPE

Hope Is the Thing with Feathers

Hope is the thing with feathers
That perches in the soul,
And sings the tune without the words,
And never stops at all,

And sweetest in the gale is heard;
And sore must be the storm
That could abash the little bird
That kept so many warm.

I've heard it in the chillest land,
And on the strangest sea;
Yet, never, in extremity,
It asked a crumb of me.

EMILY DICKINSON

Work Without Hope

All Nature seems at work. Slugs leave their lair—
The bees are stirring—birds are on the wing—
And Winter, slumbering in the open air,
Wears on his smiling face a dream of Spring!
And I, the while, the sole unbusy thing,
Nor honey make, nor pair, nor build, nor sing.

Yet well I ken the banks where amaranths blow,
Have traced the fount whence streams of nectar flow.
Bloom, O ye amaranths! bloom for whom ye may,
For me ye bloom not! Glide, rich streams, away!
With lips unbrighten'd, wreathless brow, I stroll:
And would you learn the spells that drowse my soul?
Work without Hope draws nectar in a sieve,
And Hope without an object cannot live.

SAMUEL TAYLOR COLERIDGE

The Rainy Day

The day is cold, and dark, and dreary;
It rains, and the wind is never weary;
The vine still clings to the moldering wall,
But at every gust the dead leaves fall,
  And the day is dark and dreary.

My life is cold, and dark, and dreary;
It rains, and the wind is never weary;
My thoughts still cling to the moldering Past,
But the hopes of youth fall thick in the blast
  And the days are dark and dreary.

Be still, sad heart! and cease repining;
Behind the clouds is the sun still shining;
  Thy fate is the common fate of all,
Into each life some rain must fall,
  Some days must be dark and dreary.

HENRY WADSWORTH LONGFELLOW

Song

Love laid his sleepless head
On a thorny rosy bed;
And his eyes with tears were red,
And pale his lips as the dead.

And fear and sorrow and scorn
Kept watch by his head forlorn,
Till the night was overworn,
And the world was merry with morn.

And Joy came up with the day,
And kissed Love's lips as he lay,
And the watchers ghostly and gray
Sped from his pillow away.

And his eyes as the dawn grew bright,
And his lips waxed ruddy as light:
Sorrow may reign for a night,
But day shall bring back delight.

ALGERNON CHARLES SWINBURNE

HUMANITY

I Am the People, the Mob

I am the people—the mob—the crowd—the mass.
Do you know that all the great work of the world is done
through me?
I am the workingman, the inventor, the maker of the
world's food and clothes.
I am the audience that witnesses history. The Napoleons
come from me and the Lincolns. They die. And then I
send forth more Napoleons and Lincolns.
I am the seed ground. I am a prairie that will stand for much
plowing. Terrible storms pass over me. I forget. The best
of me is sucked out and wasted. I forget. Everything but
Death comes to me and makes me work and give up what
I have. And I forget.

Sometimes I growl, shake myself and spatter a few red drops for history to remember. Then—I forget.

When I, the People, learn to remember, when I, the People, use the lessons of yesterday and no longer forget who robbed me last year, who played me for a fool—then there will be no speaker in all the world say the name: "The People," with any fleck of a sneer in his voice or any far-off smile of derision.

The mob—the crowd—the mass—will arrive then.

CARL SANDBURG

My Days Among the Dead

My days among the dead are past;
  Around me I behold,
Wher'er these casual eyes are cast,
  The mighty minds of old:
My never-failing friends are they,
With whom I converse day by day.

With them I take delight in weal
  And seek relief in woe;
And while I understand and feel
  How much to them I owe,
My cheeks have often been bedewed
With tears of thoughtful gratitude.

My thoughts are with the Dead; with them
  I live in long-past years,
Their virtues love, their faults condemn,
  Partake their hopes and fears;
And from their lessons seek and find
Instruction with an humble mind.

My hopes are with the Dead; anon
   My place with them will be,
And I with them shall travel on
   Through all Futurity;
Yet leaving here a name, I trust,
That will not perish in the dust.

ROBERT SOUTHEY

from *An Essay on Man*

Know then thyself, presume not God to scan,
The proper study of mankind is man.
Placed on this isthmus of a middle state,
A being darkly wise, and rudely great:
With too much knowledge for the sceptic side,
With too much weakness for the stoic's pride,
He hangs between; in doubt to act, or rest;
In doubt to deem himself a god, or beast;
In doubt his mind or body to prefer;
Born but to die, and reasoning but to err;
Alike in ignorance, his reason such,
Whether he thinks too little or too much:
Chaos of thought and passion, all confused;
Still by himself abused or disabused;
Created half to rise and half to fall;
Great lord of all things, yet a prey to all;
Sole judge of truth, in endless error hurled:
The glory, jest, and riddle of the world!

ALEXANDER POPE

The Dead

I see them,—crowd on crowd they walk the earth,
Dry leafless trees no autumn wind laid bare;
And in their nakedness find cause for mirth,
And all unclad would winter's rudeness dare;
No sap doth through their clattering branches flow,
Whence springing leaves and blossoms bright appear;
Their hearts the living God have ceased to know
Who gives the spring-time to th' expectant year.
They mimic life, as if from Him to steal
His glow of health to paint the livid cheek;
They borrow words for thoughts they cannot feel,
That with a seeming heart their tongue may speak;
And in their show of life more dead they live
Than those that to the earth with many tears they give.

JONES VERY

152

Four Seasons Fill the Measure

Four seasons fill the measure of the year;
There are four seasons in the mind of man:
He has his lusty Spring, when fancy clear
Takes in all beauty with an easy span:
He has his Summer, when luxuriously
Spring's honey'd cud of youthful thought he loves
To ruminate, and by such dreaming nigh
His nearest unto heaven: quiet coves
His soul has in its Autumn, when his wings
He furleth close: contented so to look
On mists in idleness—to let fair things
Pass by unheeded as a threshold brook:
He has his Winter too of pale misfeature,
Or else he would forgo his mortal nature.

JOHN KEATS

IMAGINATION

Aladdin

When I was a beggarly boy,
  And lived in a cellar damp,
I had not a friend nor a toy,
  But I had Aladdin's lamp;
When I could not sleep for the cold,
  I had fire enough in my brain,
And builded, with roofs of gold,
  My beautiful castles in Spain!

Since then I have toiled day and night,
  I have money and power good store,
But I'd give all my lamps of silver bright
  For the one that is mine no more.
Take, Fortune, whatever you choose;
  You gave and may snatch again;
I have nothing 'twould pain me to lose,
  For I own no more castles in Spain!

JAMES RUSSELL LOWELL

Song

Go and catch a falling star,
  Get with child a mandrake root,
Tell me where all past years are,
  Or who cleft the devil's foot,
Teach me to hear mermaids singing,
Or to keep off envy's stinging,
        And find what wind
Serves to advance an honest mind.

If thou beest born to strange sights,
  Things invisible to see,
Ride ten thousand days and nights,
  Till age snow white hairs on thee,
Thou, when thou return'st, wilt tell me
All strange wonders that befell thee,
        And swear no where
Lives a woman true and fair.

If thou find'st one, let me know;
   Such a pilgrimage were sweet.
Yet do not, I would not go,
   Though at next door we might meet.

Though she were true when you met her,
And last till you write your letter,
         Yet she will be
False, ere I come, to two or three.

                              JOHN DONNE

Oread

Whirl up, sea—
Whirl your pointed pines.
Splash your great pines
On our rocks.
Hurl your green over us—
Cover us with your pools of fir.

H. D.

I Wandered Lonely As a Cloud

I wandered lonely as a cloud
That floats on high o'er vales and hills,
When all at once I saw a crowd,
A host, of golden daffodils;
Beside the lake, beneath the trees,
Fluttering and dancing in the breeze.

Continuous as the stars that shine
And twinkle on the milky way,
They stretched in never-ending line
Along the margin of a bay:
Ten thousand saw I at a glance,
Tossing their heads in sprightly dance.

The waves beside them danced; but they
Out-did the sparkling waves in glee:
A poet could not but be gay,
In such a jocund company:
I gazed—and gazed—but little thought
What wealth the show to me had brought:

For oft, when on my couch I lie
In vacant or in pensive mood,
They flash upon that inward eye
Which is the bliss of solitude;
And then my heart with pleasure fills,
And dances with the daffodils.

WILLIAM WORDSWORTH

Anyone Lived in a Pretty How Town

anyone lived in a pretty how town
(with up so floating many bells down)
spring summer autumn winter
he sang his didn't he danced his did.

Women and men(both little and small)
cared for anyone not at all
they sowed their isn't they reaped their same
sun moon stars rain

children guessed(but only a few
and down they forgot as up they grew
autumn winter spring summer)
that noone loved him more by more

when by now and tree by leaf
she laughed his joy she cried his grief
bird by snow and stir by still
anyone's any was all to her

someones married their everyones
laughed their cryings and did their dance
(sleep wake hope and then)they
said their nerves they slept their dream

stars rain sun moon
(and only the snow can begin to explain
how children are apt to forget to remember
with up so floating many bells down)

one day anyone died i guess
(and noone stooped to kiss his face)
busy folk buried them side by side
little by little and was by was

all by all and deep by deep
and more by more they dream their sleep
noone and anyone earth by april
wish by spirit and if by yes.

Woman and men(both dong and ding)
summer autumn winter spring
reaped their sowing and went their came
sun moon stars rain

e. e. cummings

The Emperor of Ice-Cream

Call the roller of big cigars,
The muscular one, and bid him whip
In kitchen cups concupiscent curds.
Let the wenches dawdle in such dress
As they are used to wear, and let the boys
Bring flowers in last month's newspapers.
Let be be finale of seem.
The only emperor is the emperor of ice-cream.

Take from the dresser of deal,
Lacking the three glass knobs, that sheet
On which she embroidered fantails once
And spread it so as to cover her face.
If her horny feet protrude, they come
To show how cold she is, and dumb.
Let the lamp affix its beam.
The only emperor is the emperor of ice-cream.

WALLACE STEVENS

JOURNEYS

The Ocean of Life

Ships that pass in the night, and speak
   each other in passing;
Only a signal shown and a distant
   voice in the darkness;
So in the ocean of life we pass and
   speak one another,
Only a look and a voice; then darkness
   again and a silence.

HENRY WADSWORTH LONGFELLOW

Sailing to Byzantium

I

That is no country for old men. The young
In one another's arms, birds in the trees
—Those dying generations—at their song,
The salmon-falls, the mackerel-crowded seas,
Fish, flesh, or fowl, commend all summer long
Whatever is begotten, born, and dies.
Caught in that sensual music all neglect
Monuments of unageing intellect.

II

An aged man is but a paltry thing,
A tattered coat upon a stick, unless
Soul clap its hands and sing, and louder sing
For every tatter in its mortal dress,
Nor is there singing school but studying
Monuments of its own magnificence;
And therefore I have sailed the seas and come
To the holy city of Byzantium.

III

O sages standing in God's holy fire
As in the gold mosaic of a wall,
Come from the holy fire, perne in a gyre,
And be the singing-masters of my soul.
Consume my heart away; sick with desire
And fastened to a dying animal
It knows not what it is; and gather me
Into the artifice of eternity.

IV

Once out of nature I shall never take
My bodily form from any natural thing,
But such a form as Grecian goldsmiths make
Of hammered gold and gold enamelling
To keep a drowsy Emperor awake;
Or set upon a golden bough to sing
To lords and ladies of Byzantium
Of what is past, or passing, or to come.

WILLIAM BUTLER YEATS

The Tide Rises, the Tide Falls

The tide rises, the tide falls,
The twilight darkens, the curfew calls;
Along the sea-sands damp and brown
The traveller hastens toward the town,
   And the tide rises, the tide falls.

Darkness settles on roofs and walls,
But the sea, the sea in the darkness calls;
The little waves, with their soft, white hands,
Efface the footprints in the sands,
   And the tide rises, the tide falls.

The morning breaks; the steeds in their stalls
Stamp and neigh, as the hostler calls;
The day returns, but nevermore
Returns the traveller to the shore,
   And the tide rises, the tide falls.

HENRY WADSWORTH LONGFELLOW

Up-hill

Does the road wind up-hill all the way?
　　Yes, to the very end.
Will the day's journey take the whole long day?
　　From morn to night, my friend.

But is there for the night a resting-place?
　　A roof for when the slow dark hours begin.
May not the darkness hide it from my face?
　　You cannot miss that inn.

Shall I meet other wayfarers at night?
　　Those who have gone before.
Then must I knock, or call when just in sight?
　　They will not keep you standing at that door.

Shall I find comfort, travel-sore and weak?
　　Of labour you shall find the sum.
Will there be beds for me and all who seek?
　　Yea, beds for all who come.

CHRISTINA ROSSETTI

JOY

A Birthday

My heart is like a singing bird
  Whose nest is in a watered shoot:
My heart is like an apple tree
  Whose boughs are bent with thickset fruit;
My heart is like a rainbow shell
  That paddles in a halcyon sea;
My heart is gladder than all these
  Because my love is come to me.

Raise me a dais of silk and down;
  Hang it with vair and purple dyes;
Carve it in doves and pomegranates,
  And peacocks with a hundred eyes;
Work it in gold and silver grapes,
  In leaves and silver fleurs-de-lys;
Because the birthday of my life
  Is come, my love is come to me.

CHRISTINA ROSSETTI

168

To a Skylark

Hail to thee, blithe Spirit!
   Bird thou never wert,
That from Heaven, or near it,
   Pourest thy full heart
In profuse strains of unpremeditated art.

   Higher still and higher
   From the earth thou springest
Like a cloud of fire;
   The blue deep thou wingest,
And singing still dost soar, and soaring ever singest.

   In the golden lightning
   Of the sunken sun,
O'er which clouds are bright'ning,
   Thou dost float and run;
Like an unbodied joy whose race is just begun.

   The pale purple even
   Melts around thy flight;
Like a star of Heaven,
   In the broad daylight
Thou art unseen, but yet I hear thy shrill delight,

Keen as are the arrows
    Of that silver sphere,
Whose intense lamp narrows
    In the white dawn clear
Until we hardly see—we feel that it is there.

All the earth and air
    With thy voice is loud,
As when night is bare,
    From one lonely cloud
The moon rains out her beams, and
        Heaven is overflowed.

What thou art we know not;
    What is most like thee?
From rainbow clouds there flow not
    Drops so bright to see
As from thy presence showers a rain of melody.

Like a Poet hidden
    In the light of thought,
Singing hymns unbidden,
    Till the world is wrought
To sympathy with hopes and fears it heeded not:

Like a high-born maiden
    In a palace-tower,
Soothing her love-laden
    Soul in secret hour
With music sweet as love, which overflows her bower:

Like a glow-worm golden
    In a dell of dew,
Scattering unbeholden
    Its aëreal hue
Among the flowers and grass, which screen it from the
    view!

Like a rose embowered
    In its own green leaves,
By warm winds deflowered,
    Till the scent it gives
Makes faint with too much sweet those heavy-wingéd
    thieves:

Sound of vernal showers
    On the twinkling grass,
Rain-awakened flowers,
    All that ever was
Joyous, and clear, and fresh, thy music doth surpass:

Teach us, Sprite or Bird,
    What sweet thoughts are thine:
I have never heard
    Praise of love or wine
That panted forth a flood of rapture so divine.

Chorus Hymeneal,
    Or triumphal chant,
Matched with thine would be all
    But an empty vaunt,
A thing wherein we feel there is some hidden want.

What objects are the fountains
    Of thy happy strain?
What fields, or waves, or mountains?
    What shapes of sky or plain?
What love of thine own kind? what ignorance of pain?

With thy clear keen joyance
    Languor cannot be:
Shadow of annoyance
    Never came near thee:
Thou lovest—but ne'er knew love's sad satiety.

Waking or asleep,
    Thou of death must deem
Things more true and deep
    Than we mortals dream.
Or how could thy notes flow in such a crystal stream?

We look before and after,
    And pine for what is not:
Our sincerest laughter
    With some pain is fraught;
Our sweetest songs are those that tell of saddest thought.

    Yet if we could scorn
        Hate, and pride, and fear;
    If we were things born
        Not to shed a tear,
I know not how thy joy we ever should come near.

    Better than all measures
        Of delightful sound,
    Better than all treasures
        That in books are found,
Thy skill to poet were, thou scorner of the ground!

    Teach me half the gladness
        That thy brain must know,
    Such harmonious madness
        From my lips would flow
The world should listen then—as I am listening now.

PERCY BYSSHE SHELLEY

Daybreak

A Wind came up out of the sea,
And said, "O mists, make room for me."

It hailed the ships, and cried, "Sail on,
Ye mariners, the night is gone."

And hurried landward far away,
Crying, "Awake! it is the day."

It said unto the forest, "Shout!
Hang all your leafy banners out!"

It touched the wood-bird's folded wing,
And said, "O bird, awake and sing."

And o'er the farms, "O chanticleer,
Your clarion blow; the day is near."

It whispered to the fields of corn,
"Bow down, and hail the coming morn."

It shouted through the belfry tower,
"Awake, O bell! proclaim the hours."

It crossed the churchyard with a sigh,
And said, "Not yet! in quiet lie."

HENRY WADSWORTH LONGFELLOW

Commonplace

"A commonplace life," we say, and we sigh,
But why should we sigh as we say?
The commonplace sun in the commonplace sky
Makes up the commonplace day;
The moon and the stars are commonplace things,
And the flower that blooms, and the bird that sings,
But dark were the world, and sad our lot,
If the flowers failed, and the sun shone not;
And God, who studies each separate soul,
Out of commonplace lives makes His beautiful whole.

SUSAN COOLIDGE

He Hears with Gladdened Heart the Thunder

He hears with gladdened heart the thunder
   Peal, and loves the falling dew;
He knows the earth above and under—
   Sits and is content to view.

He sits beside the dying ember,
   God for hope and man for friend,
Content to see, glad to remember,
   Expectant of the certain end.

ROBERT LOUIS STEVENSON

LIVE FOR
TODAY

To His Coy Mistress

Had we but world enough, and time,
This coyness, lady, were no crime.
We would sit down, and think which way
To walk, and pass our long love's day.
Thou by the Indian Ganges' side
Shouldst rubies find: I by the tide
Of Humber would complain. I would
Love you ten years before the flood,
And you should, if you please, refuse
Till the conversion of the Jews;
My vegetable love should grow
Vaster than empires and more slow;
An hundred years should go to praise
Thine eyes, and on thy forehead gaze;

Two hundred to adore each breast,
But thirty thousand to the rest;
An age at least to every part,
And the last age should show your heart.
For, lady, you deserve this state;
Nor would I love at lower rate.
But at my back I always hear
Time's wingéd chariot hurrying near;
And yonder all before us lie
Deserts of vast eternity.
Thy beauty shall no more be found,
Nor in thy marble vault shall sound
My echoing song; then worms shall try
That long preserved virginity;
And your quaint honor turn to dust,
And into ashes all my lust:
The grave's a fine and private place,
But none, I think, do there embrace.

Now therefore, while the youthful hue
Sits on thy skin like morning dew,
And while thy willing soul transpires
At every pore with instant fires,
Now let us sport us while we may,
And now, like amorous birds of prey,
Rather at once our time devour
Than languish in his slow-chapped power,
Let us roll all our strength and all
Our sweetness up into one ball,

And tear our pleasures with rough strife
Thorough the iron gates of life:
Thus, though we cannot make our sun
Stand still, yet we will make him run.

ANDREW MARVELL

O to Be Up and Doing

O to be up and doing,
Unfearing and unashamed to go
In all the uproar and the press
About my human business!
My undissuaded heart I hear
Whisper courage in my ear.
With voiceless calls, the ancient earth
Summons me to a daily birth,
Thou, O my love, ye, O my friends—
The gist of life, the end of ends—
To laugh, to love, to live, to die
Ye call me by the ear and eye!

ROBERT LOUIS STEVENSON

Come Down, O Maid

"Come down, O maid, from yonder mountain height:
What pleasure lives in height (the shepherd sang),
In height and cold, the splendour of the hills?
But cease to move so near the Heavens, and cease
To glide a sunbeam by the blasted Pine,
To sit a star upon the sparkling spire:
And come, for Love is of the valley, come,
For Love is of the valley, come thou down
And find him; by the happy threshold, he,
Or hand in hand with Plenty in the maize,
Or red with spirited purple of the vats,
Or foxlike in the vine; or cares to walk
With Death and Morning on the silver horns,
Nor wilt thou snare him in the white ravine,
Nor find him dropt upon the firths of ice,
That huddling slant in furrow-cloven falls
To roll the torrent out of dusky doors:
But follow: let the torrent dance thee down
To find him in the valley; let the wild
Lean-headed Eagles yelp alone, and leave
The monstrous ledges there to slope, and spill
Their thousand wreaths of dangling watersmoke,

That like a broken purpose waste in air:
So waste not thou: but come; for all the vales
Await thee: azure pillars of the hearth
Arise to thee: the children call, and I
Thy shepherd pipe, and sweet is every sound,
Sweeter thy voice, but every sound is sweet;
Myriads of rivulets hurry thro' the lawn,
The moan of doves in immemorial elms,
And murmuring of innumerable bees."

ALFRED, LORD TENNYSON

Away with Funeral Music

Away with funeral music—set
The pipe to powerful lips—
The cup of life's for him that drinks
And not for him that sips.

ROBERT LOUIS STEVENSON

What Is to Come

What is to come we know not. But we know
That what has been was good—was good to show,
Better to hide, and best of all to bear.
We are the masters of the days that were;
We have lived, we have loved, we have suffered . . . even so

Shall we not take the ebb who had the flow?
Life was our friend. Now, if it be our foe—
Dear, though it spoil and break us!—need we care
      What is to come?
Let the great winds their worst and wildest blow,
Or the gold weather round us mellow slow;
We have fulfilled ourselves, and we can dare
And we can conquer, though we may not share
In the rich quiet of the afterglow
      What is to come.

WILLIAM ERNEST HENLEY

Gather Ye Roses

Gather ye roses while ye may,
   Old time is still a-flying;
A world where beauty fleets away
   Is no world for denying.
Come lads and lasses, fall to play
   Lose no more time in sighing.

The very flowers you pluck to-day
   To-morrow will be dying;
   And all the flowers are crying,
And all the leaves have tongues to say,—
Gather ye roses while ye may.

ROBERT LOUIS STEVENSON

Glycine's Song

A sunny shaft did I behold,
From sky to earth it slanted:
And poised therein a bird so bold—
Sweet bird, thou wert enchanted!
He sank, he rose, he twinkled, he troll'd
Within that shaft of sunny mist;
His eyes of fire, his beak of gold,
All else of amethyst!

And thus he sang: 'Adieu! adieu!
Love's dreams prove seldom true.
The blossoms, they make no delay:
The sparking dew-drops will not stay.
  Sweet month of May,
    We must away;
    Far, far away!
      To-day! to-day!'

SAMUEL TAYLOR COLERIDGE

LOVE

My Luve

O my luve is like a red, red rose,
   That's newly sprung in June:
O my luve is like the melodie,
   That's sweetly played in tune.

As fair art thou, my bonie lass,
   So deep in luve am I;
And I will luve thee still, my dear,

Till a' the seas gang dry.

Till a' the seas gang dry, my dear,
  And the rocks melt wi' the sun:
And I will luve thee still, my dear,
  While the sands o' life shall run.

And fare thee weel, my only luve!
  And fare thee weel a while!
And I will come again, my luve,
  Tho' it were ten thousand mile.

ROBERT BURNS

Ruth 1:16-18

And Ruth said, Intreat me not to leave
thee, or to return from following after thee:
for whither thou goest, I will go; and where
thou lodgest, I will lodge: thy people shall be
my people, and thy God my God:

Where thou diest, will I die, and there
will I be buried: the LORD do so to me, and
more also, if ought but death part thee and
me.

Let Me Not to the
Marriage of True Minds

Let me not to the marriage of true minds
Admit impediments. Love is not love
Which alters when it alteration finds,
Or bends with the remover to remove:
O, no! it is an ever-fixed mark,
That looks on tempests and is never shaken;
It is the star to every wandering bark,
Whose worth's unknown, although his height be taken.
Love's not Time's fool, though rosy lips and cheeks
Within his bending sickle's compass come;
Love alters not with his brief hours and weeks,
But bears it out even to the edge of doom.
   If this be error, and upon me prov'd,
   I never writ, nor no man ever lov'd.

WILLIAM SHAKESPEARE

191

from *Rabbi Ben Ezra*

Grow old along with me!
The best is yet to be,
The last of life, for which the first was made:
Our times are in his hand
Who saith: "A whole I planned,
Youth shows but half; trust God, see all, nor be afraid."

Ah, but a man's reach should exceed his grasp,
Or what's a heaven for?

ROBERT BROWNING

The Bargain

My true love hath my heart, and I have his,
  By just exchange one for another given:
I hold his dear, and mine he cannot miss,
  There never was a better bargain driven:
    My true love hath my heart, and I have his.

His heart in me keeps him and me in one,
  My heart in him his thoughts and senses guides:
He loves my heart, for once it was his own,
  I cherish his because in me it bides:
    My true love hath my heart, and I have his.

SIR PHILIP SIDNEY

A Welcome

Come in the evening, or come in the morning,
Come when you're looked for, or come without warning,
Kisses and welcomes you'll find here before you,
And the oftener you come here the more I'll adore you.

THOMAS O. DAVIS

Song

Let my voice ring out and over the earth,
  Through all the grief and strife,
With a golden joy in a silver mirth:
  Thank God for life!

Let my voice swell out through the great abyss
  To the azure dome above,
With a chord of faith in the harp of bliss:
  Thank God for Love!

Let my voice ring out beneath and above,
  The whole world through,
O my Love and Life, O my Life and Love,
  Thank God for you!

JAMES THOMSON

Go from Me

Go from me. Yet I feel that I shall stand
Henceforward in thy shadow. Nevermore
Alone upon the threshold of my door
Of individual life, I shall command
The uses of my soul, nor lift my hand
Serenely in the sunshine as before,
Without the sense of that which I forbore—
Thy touch upon the palm. The widest land
Doom takes to part us, leaves thy heart in mine
With pulses that beat double. What I do
And what I dream include thee, as the wine
Must taste of its own grapes. And when I sue
God for myself, He hears that name of thine,
And sees within my eyes the tears of two.

ELIZABETH BARRETT BROWNING

Song

Come, rest in this bosom, my own stricken deer,
Though the herd have fled from thee, thy home is still
  here;
Here still is the smile, that no cloud can o'ercast,
And a heart and a hand all thy own to the last.

Oh! what was love made for, if 'tis not the same
Through joy and through torment, through glory and
  shame?
I know not, I ask not, if guilt's in that heart,
I but know that I love thee, whatever thou art.

Thou hast call'd me thy Angel in moments of bliss,
And thy Angel I'll be, 'mid the horrors of this,—
Through the furnace, unshrinking, thy steps to pursue,
And shield thee, and save thee,—or perish there too!

THOMAS MOORE

To His Lute

My lute, awake! perform the last
Labour that thou and I shall waste,
   And end that I have now begun;
For when this song is said and past,
   My lute, be still, for I have done.

As to be heard where ear is none,
As lead to grave in marble stone,
   My song may pierce her heart as soon:
Should we then sing, or sigh, or moan?
   No, no, my lute! for I have done.

The rocks do not so cruelly
Repulse the waves continually,
   As she my suit and affection:
So that I am past remedy:
   Whereby my lute and I have done.

Proud of the spoil that thou hast got
Of simple hearts thorough Love's shot,
   By whom, unkind, thou hast them won;
Think not he hath his bow forgot,
   Although my lute and I have done.

Vengeance shall fall on thy disdain,
That makest but game of earnest pain:
  Trow not alone under the sun
Unquit to cause thy lover's plain,
  Although my lute and I have done.

May chance thee lie wither'd and old
The winter nights that are so cold,
  Plaining in vain unto the moon:
Thy wishes then dare not be told:
  Care then who list! for I have done.

And then may chance thee to repent
The time that thou has lost and spent
  To cause thy lover's sigh and swoon:
Then shalt thou know beauty but lent,
  And wish and want as I have done.

Now cease, my lute! this is the last
Labour that thou and I shall waste,
  And ended is that we begun:
Now is this song both sung and past—
  My lute, be still, for I have done.

SIR THOMAS WYATT

Take Back the Heart

Take back the heart thou gavest,
What is my anguish to thee?
Take back the freedom thou cravest,
Leaving the letters to me.
Take back the words thou hast spoken.
Fling them aside and be free,
Smile o'er each pitiful token,
Leaving the sorrow to me.
Drink deep of life's fond illusion,
Gaze on the storm cloud and flee,
Swiftly through strife and confusion,
Leaving the burden to me.

Then when at last overtaken,
Time flings its fetters o'er thee,
Come with a trust still unshaken,
Come back a captive to me,
Come back in sadness or sorrow,
Once more my darling to be,
Come as of old, love, to borrow
Glimpses of sunlight from me.
Love shall resume her dominion,
Striving no more to be free,
When on her world-weary pinion,
Flies back my lost love to me.

CHARLOTTE A. BARNARD

200

Love Not Me for Comely Grace

Love not me for comely grace,
  For my pleasing eyes or face,
Nor for any outward part,
No, nor for a constant heart:
  For these may fail or turn to ill,
  So thou and I shall sever:
Keep, therefore, a true woman's eye,
And love me still but know not why—
  So hast thou the same reason still
  To dote upon me ever!

ANONYMOUS

If Thou Must Love Me

If thou must love me, let it be for naught
Except for love's sake only. Do not say,
"I love her for her smile—her look—her way
Of speaking gently,—for a trick of thought
That falls in well with mine, and certes brought
A sense of pleasant ease on such a day"—
For these things in themselves, Beloved, may
Be changed, or change for thee—and love, so wrought,
May be unwrought so. Neither love me for
Thine own dear pity's wiping my cheeks dry:
A creature might forget to weep, who bore
Thy comfort long, and lose thy love thereby!
But love me for love's sake, that evermore
Thou mayest love on, through love's eternity.

ELIZABETH BARRETT BROWNING

The Canonization

For God's sake hold your tongue, and let me love,
   Or chide my palsy, or my gout,
   My five grey hairs, or ruined fortune flout;
With wealth your state, your mind with arts improve,
     Take you a course, get you a place,
     Observe his Honor, or his Grace;
Or the king's real, or his stamped face
   Contemplate; what you will, approve,
   So you will let me love.

Alas, alas, who's injured by my love?
   What merchant's ships have my sighs drowned?
   Who says my tears have overflowed his ground?
When did my colds a forward spring remove?
     When did the heats which my veins fill
     Add one more to the plaguy bill?
Soldiers find wars, and lawyers find out still
   Litigious men, which quarrels move,
   Though she and I do love.

Call us what you will, we are made such by love;
   Call her one, me another fly,
   We're tapers too, and at our own cost die,

And we in us find the eagle and the dove
   The phoenix riddle hath more wit
   By us; we two being one are it.
So to one neutral thing both sexes fit,
   We die and rise the same, and prove
   Mysterious by this love.

We can die by it, if not live by love,
   And if unfit for tomb or hearse
   Our legend be, it will be fit for verse;
And if no piece of chronicle we prove,
   We'll build in sonnets pretty rooms;
   As well a well-wrought urn becomes
The greatest ashes, as half-acre tombs,
   And by these hymns all shall approve
   Us canonized for love.

And thus invoke us, "You, whom reverend love
   Made one another's hermitage;
   You, to whom love was peace, that now is rage:
Who did the whole world's soul contract, and drove
   Into the glasses of your eyes
   (So made such mirrors, and such spies,
That they did all to you epitomize);
   Countries, towns, courts beg from above
   A pattern of your love."

JOHN DONNE

Appraisal

Never think she loves him wholly,
Never believe her love is blind,
All his faults are locked securely
In a closet of her mind;
All his indecisions folded
Like old flags that time has faded,
Limp and streaked with rain,
And his cautiousness like garments
Frayed and thin, with many a stain—
Let them be, oh, let them be,
There is treasure to outweigh them,
His proud will that sharply stirred,
Climbs as surely as the tide,
Senses strained too taut to sleep,
Gentleness to beast and bird,
Humor flickering hushed and wide
As the moon on moving water,
And a tenderness too deep
To be gathered in a word.

SARA TEASDALE

Love Me Little, Love Me Long

Love me little, love me long,
Is the burden of my song.
Love that is too hot and strong
　　Burneth soon to waste.
Still, I would not have thee cold,
Not too backward, nor too bold;
Love that lasteth till 'tis old
Fadeth not in haste.
　　　　Love me little, love me long,
　　　　Is the burden of my song.

If thou lovest me too much,
It will not prove as true as touch;
Love me little, more than such,
　　For I fear the end.
I am with little well content,
And a little from thee sent
Is enough, with true intent
　　To be steadfast friend.
　　　　Love me little, love me long, etc.

Say thou lov'st me while thou live;
I to thee my love will give,
Never dreaming to deceive
  Whiles that life endures.
Nay, and after death, in sooth,
I to thee will keep my truth,
As now, when in my May of youth;
  This my love assures.
    Love me little, love me long, etc.

Constant love is moderate ever,
And it will through life persever;
Give me that, with true endeavor
  I will it restore.
A suit of durance let it be
For all weathers—that for me,
For the land or for the sea,
  Lasting evermore.
    Love me little, love me long, etc.

Winter's cold, or summer's heat,
Autumn's tempests, on it beat,
It can never know defeat,
   Never can rebel.
Such the love that I would gain,
Such the love, I tell thee plain,
Thou must give, or woo in vain;
   So to thee, farewell!
     Love me little, love me long,
     Is the burden of my song.

ANONYMOUS

Love

I love you,
Not only for what you are,
But for what I am
When I am with you.
I love you,
Not only for what
You have made of yourself,
But for what
You are making of me.

I love you
For the part of me
That you bring out;
I love you
For putting your hand
Into my heaped-up heart
And passing over
All the foolish, weak things
That you can't help
Dimly seeing there,
And for drawing out
Into the light
All the beautiful belongings
That no one else had looked
Quite far enough to find.

I love you because you
Are helping me to make
Of the lumber of my life
Not a tavern
But a temple;
Out of the works
Of my every day
Not a reproach
But a song.

I love you
Because you have done
More than any creed
Could have done
To make me good,
And more than any fate
Could have done
To make me happy.
You have done it
Without a touch,
Without a word,
Without a sign.
You have done it
By being yourself,
Perhaps that is what
Being a friend means
After all.

ANONYMOUS

To My Dear and Loving Husband

If ever two were one, then surely we.
If ever man were loved by wife, then thee;
If ever wife was happy in a man,
Compare with me ye women if you can.
I prize thy love more than whole mines of gold,
Or all the riches that the East doth hold.
My love is such that rivers cannot quench,
Nor ought but love from thee give recompense.
Thy love is such I can no way repay;
The heavens reward thee manifold, I pray.
Then while we live, in love let's so persever,
That when we live no more we may live ever.

ANNE BRADSTREET

Most Like an Arch This Marriage

Most like an arch—an entrance which upholds
and shores the stone-crush up the air like lace.
Mass made idea, and idea held in place.
A lock in time. Inside half-heaven unfolds.

Most like an arch—two weaknesses that lean
into a strength. Two fallings become firm.
Two joined abeyances become a term
naming the fact that teaches fact to mean.

Not quite that? Not much less. World as it is,
what's strong and separate falters. All I do
at piling stone on stone apart from you
is roofless around nothing. Till we kiss
I am no more than upright and unset.
It is by falling in and in we make
the all-bearing point, for one another's sake,
in faultless failing, raised by our own weight.

JOHN CIARDI

My Beloved Is Mine, and I Am His

Even like two little bank-dividing brooks
  That wash the pebbles with their wanton streams,
And having ranged and searched a thousand nooks,
  Meet both at length in silver-breasted Thames,
    Where in a greater current they conjoin,
So I my best beloved's am; so he is mine.

Even so we met, and after long pursuit,
  Even so we joined; we both became entire.
No need for either to renew a suit,
  For I was flax, and he was flames of fire,
    Our firm-united souls did more than twine;
So I my best beloved's am; so he is mine.

Nor time, nor place, nor chance, nor death can bow
  My least desires unto the least remove;
He's firmly mine by oath, I his by vow;
  He's mine by faith, and I am his by love;
    He's mine by water, I am his by wine;
Thus I my best beloved's am; thus he is mine.

He is my altar; I, his holy place;
   I am his guest, and he my living food;
I'm his by penitence, he mine by grace;
   I'm his by purchase, he is mine by blood!
      He's my supporting elm, and I his vine;
Thus I my best beloved's am; thus he is mine.

He gives me wealth, I give him all my vows;
   I give him songs, he gives me length of days;
With wreaths of grace he crowns my conquering brows,
   And I his temples with a crown of praise,
      Which he accepts as an everlasting sign
That I my best beloved's am, that he is mine.

FRANCIS QUARLES

A Woman's Last Word

Let's contend no more, Love,
  Strive nor weep;
All be as before, Love,
  —Only sleep!

What so wild as words are?
  I and thou
In debate, as birds are,
  Hawk on bough!

See the creature stalking
  While we speak!
Hush and hide the talking,
  Cheek on cheek!

What so false as truth is,
  False to thee?
Where the serpent's tooth is
  Shun the tree—

Where the apple reddens
  Never pry—
Lest we lose our Edens,
  Eve and I.

Be a god and hold me
  With a charm!
Be a man and fold me
  With thine arm!

Teach me, only teach, Love!
  As I ought
I will speak thy speech, Love,
  Think thy thought—

Meet, if thou require it,
  Both demands,
Laying flesh and spirit
  In thy hands.

That shall be tomorrow
  Not tonight:
I must bury sorrow
  Out of sight:

—Must a little weep, Love,
  (Foolish me!)
And so fall asleep, Love,
  Loved by thee.

ROBERT BROWNING

When to the Sessions of Sweet Silent Thought

When to the sessions of sweet silent thought
I summon up remembrance of things past,
I sigh the lack of many a thing I sought,
And with old woes new wail my dear times' waste:
Then can I drown an eye, unus'd to flow,
For precious friends hid in death's dateless night,
And weep afresh love's long since cancell'd woe,
And moan the expense of many a vanish'd sight:
Then can I grieve at grievances foregone,
And heavily from woe to woe tell o'er
The sad account of fore-bemoaned moan,
Which I new pay as if not paid before.
   But if the while I think on thee, dear friend,
   All losses are restor'd and sorrows end.

WILLIAM SHAKESPEARE

My Lost Youth

Often I think of the beautiful town
   That is seated by the sea;
Often in thought go up and down
The pleasant streets of that dear old town,
   And my youth comes back to me.
      And a verse of a Lapland song
      Is haunting my memory still:
      "A boy's will is the wind's will,
And the thoughts of youth are long, long thoughts."

I can see the shadowy lines of its trees,
   And catch, in sudden gleams,
The sheen of the far-surrounding seas,
And islands that were the Hesperides
   Of all my boyish dreams.
      And the burden of that old song,
      It murmurs and whispers still:
      "A boy's will is the wind's will,
And the thoughts of youth are long, long thoughts."

I remember the black wharves and the slips,
   And the sea-tides tossing free;
And Spanish sailors with bearded lips,
And the beauty and mystery of the ships,
   And the magic of the sea.
      And the voice of that wayward song
      Is singing and saying still:
      "A boy's will is the wind's will,
And the thoughts of youth are long, long thoughts."

I remember the bulwarks by the shore,
   And the fort upon the hill;
The sunrise gun, with its hollow roar,
The drum-beat repeated o'er and o'er,
   And the bugle wild and shrill.
      And the music of that old song
      Throbs in my memory still:
      "A boy's will is the wind's will,
And the thoughts of youth are long, long thoughts."

I remember the sea-fight far away,
   How it thundered o'er the tide!
And the dead captains, as they lay
In their graves, o'erlooking the tranquil bay
   Where they in battle died.
      And the sound of that mournful song
      Goes through me with a thrill:
      "A boy's will is the wind's will,
And the thoughts of youth are long, long thoughts."

I can see the breezy dome of groves,
  The shadows of Deering's Woods;
And the friendships old and the early loves
Come back with a Sabbath sound, as of doves
  In quiet neighborhoods.
      And the verse of that sweet old song,
      It flutters and murmurs still:
      "A boy's will is the wind's will,
And the thoughts of youth are long, long thoughts."

I remember the gleams and glooms that dart
  Across the school-boy's brain;
The song and the silence in the heart,
That in part are prophecies, and in part
  Are longings wild and vain.
      And the voice of that fitful song
      Sings on, and is never still:
      "A boy's will is the wind's will,
And the thoughts of youth are long, long thoughts."

There are things of which I may not speak;
  There are dreams that cannot die;
There are thoughts that make the strong heart weak,
And bring a pallor into the cheek,
  And a mist before the eye.
      And the words of that fatal song
      Come over me like a chill:
      "A boy's will is the wind's will,
And the thoughts of youth are long, long thoughts."

Strange to me now are the forms I meet
  When I visit the dear old town;
But the native air is pure and sweet,
And the trees that o'ershadow each well-known street,
  As they balance up and down,
    Are singing the beautiful song,
    Are sighing and whispering still:
    "A boy's will is the wind's will,
And the thoughts of youth are long, long thoughts."

And Deering's Woods are fresh and fair,
  And with joy that is almost pain
My heart goes back to wander there,
And among the dreams of the days that were,
  I find my lost youth again.
    And the strange and beautiful song,
    The groves are repeating it still:
    "A boy's will is the wind's will,
And the thoughts of youth are long, long thoughts."

HENRY WADSWORTH LONGFELLOW

The Coliseum

Type of the antique Rome! Rich reliquary
Of lofty contemplation left to Time
By buried centuries of pomp and power!
At length—at length—after so many days
Of weary pilgrimage and burning thirst
(Thirst for the springs of lore that in thee lie),
I kneel, an altered and an humble man,
Amid thy shadows, and so drink within
My very soul thy grandeur, gloom, and glory!
Vastness! and Age! and Memories of Eld!
Silence! and Desolation! and dim Night!
I feel ye now—I feel ye in your strength—
O spells more sure than e'er Judaean king
Taught in the gardens of Gethsemane!
O charms more potent than the rapt Chaldee
Ever drew down from out the quiet stars!

Here, where a hero fell, a column falls!
Here, where a mimic eagle glared in gold,
A midnight vigil holds the swarthy bat!
Here, where the dames of Rome their gilded hair
Waved to the wind, now wave the reed and thistle!
Here, where on golden throne the monarch lolled,
Glides, spectre-like, unto his marble home,
Lit by the wan light of the hornèd moon,
The swift and silent lizard of the stones!

But stay! these walls—these ivy-clad arcades—
These mouldering plinths—these sad and blackened
  shafts—
These vague entablatures—this crumbling frieze—
These shattered cornices—this wreck—this ruin—
These stones—alas! these gray stones—are they all—
All of the famed, and the colossal left
By the corrosive Hours to Fate and me?

"Not all"—the Echoes answer me—"not all!
Prophetic sounds and loud arise forever
From us, and from all Ruin, unto the wise,
As melody from Memnon to the Sun.
We rule the hearts of mightiest men—we rule
With a despotic sway all giant minds.
We are not impotent—we pallid stones.
Not all our power is gone—not all our fame—
Not all the magic of our high renown—
Not all the wonder that encircles us—
Not all the mysteries that in us lie—
Not all the memories that hang upon
And cling around about us as a garment,
Clothing us in a robe of more than glory."

EDGAR ALLAN POE

The Past

Thou unrelenting Past!
Strong are the barriers round thy dark domain,
   And fetters, sure and fast,
Hold all that enter thy unbreathing reign.

   Far in thy realm withdrawn,
Old empires sit in sullenness and gloom,
   And glorious ages gone
Lie deep within the shadow of thy womb.

   Childhood, with all its mirth,
Youth, Manhood, Age that draws us to the ground,
   And last, Man's Life on earth,
Glide to thy dim dominions, and are bound.

   Thou hast my better years;
Thou hast my earlier friends, the good, the kind,
   Yielded to thee with tears—
The venerable form, the exalted mind.

My spirit yearns to bring
The lost ones back—yearns with desire intense,
    And struggles hard to wring
Thy bolts apart, and pluck thy captives thence.

    In vain; thy gates deny
All passage save to those who hence depart;
    Nor to the streaming eye
Thou giv'st them back—nor to the broken heart.

    In the abysses hide
Beauty and excellence unknown; to thee
    Earth's wonder and her pride
Are gathered, as the waters to the sea;

    Labors of good to man,
Unpublished charity, unbroken faith,
    Love, that midst grief began,
And grew with years, and faltered not in death.

    Full many a mighty name
Lurks in thy depths, unuttered, unrevered;
    With thee are silent fame,
Forgotten arts, and wisdom disappeared.

Thine for a space are they—
Yet shalt thou yield thy treasures up at last:
　　Thy gates shall yet give way,
Thy bolts shall fall, inexorable Past!

　　All that of good and fair
Has gone into thy womb from earliest time,
　　Shall then come forth to wear
The glory and the beauty of its prime.

　　They have not perished—no!
Kind words, remembered voices once so sweet,
　　Smiles, radiant long ago,
And features, the great soul's apparent seat.

　　All shall come back; each tie
Of pure affection shall be knit again;
　　Alone shall Evil die,
And Sorrow dwell a prisoner in thy reign.

　　And then shall I behold
Him, by whose kind paternal side I sprung,
　　And her, who, still and cold,
Fills the next grave—the beautiful and young.

WILLIAM CULLEN BRYANT

MYSTERY

Flower in the Crannied Wall

Flower in the crannied wall,
I pluck you out of the crannies,
I hold you here, root and all, in my hand,
Little flower—but if I could understand
What you are, root and all, and all in all,
I should know what God and man is.

ALFRED, LORD TENNYSON

In a Dark Time

In a dark time, the eye begins to see,
I meet my shadow in the deepening shade;
I hear my echo in the echoing wood—
A lord of nature weeping to a tree.
I live between the heron and the wren,
Beasts of the hill and serpents of the den.

What's madness but nobility of soul
At odds with circumstance? The day's on fire!
I know the purity of pure despair,
My shadow pinned against a sweating wall.
That place among the rocks—is it a cave,
Or winding path? The edge is what I have.

A steady storm of correspondences!
A night flowing with birds, a ragged moon,
And in broad day the midnight come again!
A man goes far to find out what he is—
Death of the self in a long, tearless night,
All natural shapes blazing unnatural light.

Dark, dark my light, and darker my desire.
My soul, like some heat-maddened summer fly,
Keeps buzzing at the sill. Which I is I?
A fallen man, I climb out of my fear.
The mind enters itself, and God the mind,
And one is One, free in the tearing wind.

THEODORE ROETHKE

NATURE

Inscription for the Entrance to a Wood

Stranger, if thou hast learned a truth which needs
No school of long experience, that the world
Is full of guilt and misery, and hast seen
Enough of all its sorrows, crimes, and cares,
To tire thee of it, enter this wild wood
And view the haunts of Nature. The calm shade
Shall bring a kindred calm, and the sweet breeze
That makes the green leaves dance, shall waft a balm
To thy sick heart. Thou wilt find nothing here
Of all that pained thee in the haunts of men,
And made thee loathe thy life. The primal curse
Fell, it is true, upon the unsinning earth,
But not in vengeance. God hath yoked to guilt
Her pale tormentor, misery. Hence, these shades
Are still the abodes of gladness; the thick roof
Of green and stirring branches is alive

And musical with birds, that sing and sport
In wantonness of spirit; while below
The squirrel, with raised paws and form erect,
Chirps merrily. Throngs of insects in the shade
Try their thin wings and dance in the warm beam
That waked them into life. Even the green trees
Partake the deep contentment; as they bend
To the soft winds, the sun from the blue sky
Looks in and sheds a blessing on the scene.
Scarce less the cleft-born wild-flower seems to enjoy
Existence than the wingèd plunderer
That sucks its sweets. The mossy rocks themselves,
And the old and ponderous trunks of prostrate trees
That lead from knoll to knoll a causey rude
Or bridge the sunken brook, and their dark roots,
With all their earth upon them, twisting high,
Breathe fixed tranquillity. The rivulet
Sends forth glad sounds, and tripping o'er its bed
Of pebbly sands, or leaping down the rocks,
Seems, with continuous laughter, to rejoice
In its own being. Softly tread the marge,
Lest from her midway perch thou scare the wren
That dips her bill in water. The cool wind,
That stirs the stream in play, shall come to thee,
Like one that loves thee nor will let thee pass
Ungreeted, and shall give its light embrace.

WILLIAM CULLEN BRYANT

Song from *Pippa Passes*

The year's at the spring,
And day's at the morn;
Morning's at seven;
The hill-side's dew-pearled;
Th lark's on the wing;
The snail's on the thorn;
God's in His Heaven—
All's right with the world!

ROBERT BROWNING

The Snow-Storm

Announced by all the trumpets of the sky,
Arrives the snow, and, driving o'er the fields,
Seems nowhere to alight: the whited air
Hides hills and woods, the river, and the heaven,
And veils the farm-house at the garden's end.
The sled and traveller stopped, the courier's feet
Delayed, all friends shut out, the housemates sit
Around the radiant fireplace, enclosed
In a tumultuous privacy of storm.

Come see the north wind's masonry.
Out of an unseen quarry evermore
Furnished with tile, the fierce artificer
Curves his white bastions with projected roof
Round every windward stake, or tree, or door.
Speeding, the myriad-handed, his wild work
So fanciful, so savage, nought cares he
For number or proportion. Mockingly,
On coop or kennel he hangs Parian wreaths;
A swan-like form invests the hidden thorn;
Fills up the farmer's lane from wall to wall,
Maugre the farmer's sighs; and, at the gate,
A tapering turret overtops the work.
And when his hours are numbered, and the world
Is all his own, retiring, as he were not,

Leaves, when the sun appears, astonished Art
To mimic in slow structures, stone by stone,
Built in an age, the mad wind's night-work,
The frolic architecture of the snow.

RALPH WALDO EMERSON

On the Grasshopper and Cricket

The poetry of earth is never dead:
   When all the birds are faint with the hot sun.
   And hide in cooling trees, a voice will run
From hedge to hedge about the new-mown mead;
That is the grasshopper's—he takes the lead
   In summer luxury,—he has never done
   With his delights, for when tired out with fun
He rests at ease beneath some pleasant weed.
The poetry of earth is ceasing never:
   On a lone winter evening, when the frost
Has wrought a silence, from the stove there shrills
The cricket's song, in warmth increasing ever,
   And seems to one, in drowsiness half-lost,
The grasshopper's among some grassy hills.

JOHN KEATS

The Lamb

Little Lamb, who made thee?
Dost thou know who made thee,
Gave thee life, and bade thee feed
By the stream and o'er the mead;
Gave thee clothing of delight,
Softest clothing, woolly, bright;
Gave thee such a tender voice,
Making all the vales rejoice?
   Little Lamb, who made thee?
   Dost thou know who made thee?

Little Lamb, I'll tell thee,
Little Lamb, I'll tell thee;
He is called by thy name,
For He calls Himself a Lamb.
He is meek, and He is mild;
He became a little child.
I a child, and thou a lamb,
We are called by His name.
   Little Lamb, God bless thee!
   Little Lamb, God bless thee.

WILLIAM BLAKE

The Tiger

Tiger! Tiger! burning bright
In the forests of the night,
What immortal hand or eye
Could frame thy fearful symmetry?

In what distant deeps or skies
Burnt the fire of thine eyes?
On what wings dare he aspire?
What the hand dare seize the fire?

And what shoulder, and what art,
Could twist the sinews of thy heart?
And when thy heart began to beat,
What dread hand? and what dread feet?

What the hammer? what the chain?
In what furnace was thy brain?
What the anvil? what dread grasp
Dare its deadly terrors clasp?

When the stars threw down their spears,
And water d heaven with their tears,
Did he smile his work to see?
Did he who made the Lamb make thee?

Tiger! Tiger! burning bright
In the forests of the night,
What immortal hand or eye,
Dare frame thy fearful symmetry?

WILLIAM BLAKE

Apparently with No Surprise

Apparently with no surprise
To any happy Flower
The Frost beheads it at its play—
In accidental power—
The blonde Assassin passes on—
The Sun proceeds unmoved
To measure off another Day
For an Approving God.

EMILY DICKINSON

Who Has Seen the Wind?

Who has seen the wind?
  Neither I nor you:
But when the leaves hang trembling,
  The wind is passing through.

Who has seen the wind?
  Neither you nor I:
But when the trees bow down their heads,
  The wind is passing by.

CHRISTINA ROSSETTI

O Sweet Spontaneous

O sweet spontaneous
earth how often have
the
doting

      fingers of
prurient philosophers pinched
and
poked

thee
,has the naughty thumb
of science prodded
thy

    beauty   how
often have religions taken
thee upon their scraggy knees
squeezing and

buffeting thee that thou mightest conceive
gods
        (but
true

to the incomparable
couch of death thy
rhythmic
lover

        thou answerest

them only with

                spring)

e. e. cummings

244

PATRIOTISM

Patriotism

Breathes there the man with soul so dead,
Who never to himself hath said,
  'This is my own, my native land!'
Whose heart hath ne'er within him burn'd
As home his footsteps he hath turn'd
  From wandering on a foreign strand?
If such there breathe, go, mark him well;
For him no minstrel raptures swell;
High though his titles, proud his name,
Boundless his wealth as wish can claim;
Despite those titles, power, and pelf,
The wretch, concentred all in self,
Living, shall forfeit fair renown,
And, doubly dying, shall go down
To the vile dust from whence he sprung,
Unwept, unhonour'd, and unsung.

SIR WALTER SCOTT

For You O Democracy

Come, I will make the continent indissoluble,
I will make the most splendid race the sun ever shone upon,
I will make divine magnetic lands,
With the love of comrades,
With the life-long love of comrades.
I will plant companionship thick as trees along all the rivers
of America, and along the shores of the great lakes, and
all over the prairies,
I will make inseparable cities with their arms about each
other's necks,
By the love of comrades,
By the manly love of comrades.

For you these from me, O Democracy, to serve you ma
femme!
For you, for you I am trilling these songs.

WALT WHITMAN

PEACE

The Epitaph

Here rests his head upon the lap of Earth
    A youth, to Fortune and to Fame unknown;
Fair Science frown'd not on his humble birth
    And Melancholy mark'd him for her own.

Large was his bounty, and his soul sincere;
    Heaven did a recompense as largely send:
He gave to Misery (all he had) a tear,
    He gain'd from Heaven ('twas all he wish'd) a friend.

No farther seek his merits to disclose,
    Or draw his frailties from their dread abode
(There they alike in trembling hope repose)
    The bosom of his Father and his God.

THOMAS GRAY

Sleeping at Last

Sleeping at last, the struggle and horror past,
Sleeping at last, the trouble and tumult over,
Cold and white, out of sight of friend and of lover,
            Sleeping at last.

No more a tired heart downcast or overcast,
No more pangs that wring or shifting fears that hover,
Sleeping at last in a dreamless sleep locked fast.

Fast asleep. Singing birds in their leafy cover
    Cannot wake her, nor shake her the gusty blast.
Under the purple thyme and the purple clover
            Sleeping at last.

CHRISTINA ROSSETTI

POETRY

Poetry

I, too, dislike it: there are things that are important beyond
   all this fiddle.
Reading it, however, with a perfect contempt for it, one
   discovers in it, after all, a place for the genuine.

   Hands that can grasp, eyes
   that can dilate, hair that can rise
      if it must, these things are important not because a

high-sounding interpretation can be put upon them but
   because they are useful. When they become so derivative
   as to become unintelligible, the same thing may be said
   for all of us, that we
      do not admire what
      we cannot understand: the bat
         holding on upside down or in quest of something to

eat, elephants pushing, a wild horse taking a roll, a tireless
wolf under a tree, the immovable critic twitching his skin
like a horse that feels a flea, the base-
ball fan, the statistician
nor is it valid
to discriminate against 'business documents and

school-books'; all these phenomena are important. One
must make a distinction however: when dragged into
prominence by half poets, the result is not poetry, nor till
the poets among us can be
'literalists of
the imagination'—above
insolence and triviality and can present

for inspection, imaginary gardens with real toads in them,
shall we have it. In the meantime, if you demand on the
one hand, the raw material of poetry in
all its rawness and
that which is on the other hand
genuine, then you are interested in poetry.

MARIANNE MOORE

Ars Poetica

A poem should be palpable and mute
As a globed fruit

Dumb
As old medallions to the thumb

Silent as the sleeve-worn stone
Of casement ledges where the moss has grown—

A poem should be wordless
As the flight of birds

+

A poem should be motionless in time
As the moon climbs

Leaving, as the moon releases
Twig by twig the night-entangled trees,

Leaving, as the moon behind the winter leaves,
Memory by memory the mind—

A poem should be motionless in time
As the moon climbs

+

A poem should be equal to:
Not true

For all the history of grief
An empty doorway and a maple leaf

For love
The leaning grasses and two lights above the sea—

A poem should not mean
But be.

ARCHIBALD MACLEISH

The Author to Her Book

Thou ill-formed offspring of my feeble brain,
Who after birth didst by my side remain,
Till snatched from thence by friends, less wise than true,
Who thee abroad, exposed to public view,
Made thee in rags, halting to th' press to trudge,
Where errors were not lessened (all may judge).
At thy return my blushing was not small,
My rambling brat (in print) should mother call,
I cast thee by as one unfit for light,
Thy visage was so irksome in my sight;
Yet being mine own, at length affection would
Thy blemishes amend, if so I could:
I washed thy face, but more defects I saw,
And rubbing off a spot still made a flaw.
I stretched thy joints to make thee even feet,
Yet still thou run'st more hobbling than is meet;
In better dress to trim thee was my mind,
But nought save homespun cloth i' th' house I find.
In this array 'mongst vulgars may'st thou roam.
In critic's hands beware thou dost not come,
And take thy way where yet thou art not known;
If for thy father asked, say thou hadst none;
And for thy mother, she alas is poor,
Which caused her thus to send thee out of door.

ANNE BRADSTREET

The Apology

Think me not unkind and rude
 That I walk alone in grove and glen;
I go to the god of the wood
 To fetch his word to men.

Tax not my sloth that I
 Fold my arms beside the brook;
Each cloud that floated in the sky
 Writes a letter in my book.

Chide me not, laborious band,
 For the idle flowers I brought;
Every aster in my hand
 Goes home loaded with a thought.

There was never mystery
 But 't is figured in the flowers;
Was never secret history
 But birds tell it in the bowers.

One harvest from thy field
 Homeward brought the oxen strong;
A second crop thine acres yield,
 Which I gather in a song.

RALPH WALDO EMERSON

The Poet

Thou, who wouldst wear the name
   Of poet mid thy brethren of mankind,
And clothe in words of flame
   Thoughts that shall live within the general mind!
Deem not the framing of a deathless lay
The pastime of a drowsy summer day.

But gather all thy powers,
   And wreak them on the verse that thou dost weave,
And in thy lonely hours,
   At silent morning or at wakeful eve,
While the warm current tingles through thy veins,
Set forth the burning words in fluent strains.

No smooth array of phrase,
   Artfully sought and ordered though it be,
Which the cold rhymer lays
   Upon his page with languid industry,
Can wake the listless pulse to livelier speed,
Or fill with sudden tears the eyes that read.

The secret wouldst thou know
   To touch the heart or fire the blood at will?
Let thine own eyes o'erflow;
   Let thy lips quiver with the passionate thrill;
Seize the great thought, ere yet its power be past,
And bind, in words, the fleet emotion fast.

Then, should thy verse appear
   Halting and harsh, and all unaptly wrought,
Touch the crude line with fear,
   Save in the moment of impassioned thought;
Then summon back the original glow, and mend
The strain with rapture that with fire was penned.

Yet let no empty gust
   Of passion find an utterance in thy lay,
A blast that whirls the dust
   Along the howling street and dies away;
But feelings of calm power and mighty sweep,
Like currents journeying through the windless deep.

Seek'st thou, in living lays,
   To limn the beauty of the earth and sky?
Before thine inner gaze
   Let all that beauty in clear vision lie;
Look on it with exceeding love, and write
The words inspired by wonder and delight.

Of tempests wouldst thou sing,
   Or tell of battles—make thyself a part
Of the great tumult; cling
   To the tossed wreck with terror in thy heart;
Scale, with the assaulting host, the rampart's height,
And strike and struggle in the thickest fight.

So shalt thou frame a lay
   That haply may endure from age to age,
And they who read shall say:
 "What witchery hangs upon this poet's page!
What art is his the written spells to find
That sway from mood to mood the willing mind!"

WILLIAM CULLEN BRYANT

God of Visions

Oh, thy bright eyes must answer now,
When Reason, with a scornful brow,
Is mocking at my overthrow;
Oh, thy sweet tongue must plead for me
And tell why I have chosen thee!

Stern Reason is to judgment come,
Arrayed in all her forms of gloom:
Wilt thou, my advocate, be dumb?
No, radiant angel, speak and say
Why I did cast the world away.

Why I have persevered to shun
The common paths that others run;
And on a strange road journeyed on,
Heedless alike of wealth and power—
Of glory's wreath and pleasure's flower.

These, once, indeed, seemed Beings divine;
And they, perchance, heard vows of mine,
And saw my offerings on their shrine;
But careless gifts are seldom prized,
And mine were worthily despised.

So, with a ready heart, I swore
To seek their altar-stone no more;
And gave my spirit to adore
Thee, ever-present, phantom thing—
My slave, my comrade, and my king.

A slave, because I rule thee still;
Incline thee to my changeful will,
And make thy influence good or ill:
A comrade, for by day and night
Thou art my intimate delight—

My darling pain that wounds and sears,
And wrings a blessing out from tears
By deadening me to real cares;
And yet, a king, though prudence well
Have taught thy subject to rebel.

And am I wrong to worship where
Faith cannot doubt, nor hope despair,
Since my own soul can grant my prayer?
Speak, God of visions, plead for me,
And tell why I have chosen thee!

EMILY BRONTË

Very Like a Whale

One thing that literature would be greatly the better for

Would be a more restricted employment by authors of simile and metaphor.

Authors of all races, be they Greeks, Romans, Teutons or Celts,

Can't seem just to say that anything is the thing it is but have to go out of their way to say that it is like something else.

What does it mean when we are told

That the Assyrian came down like a wolf on the fold?

In the first place, George Gordon Byron had had enough experience

To know that it probably wasn't just one Assyrian, it was a *lot* of Assyrians.

However, as too many arguments are apt to induce apoplexy and thus hinder longevity,

We'll let it pass as one Assyrian for the sake of brevity.

Now then, this particular Assyrian, the one whose cohorts were gleaming in purple and gold,

Just what does the poet mean when he says he came down like a wolf on the fold?

In heaven and earth more than is dreamed of in our philosophy there are a great many things,

But I don't imagine that among them there is a wolf with purple and gold cohorts or purple and gold anythings.

No, no, Lord Byron, before I'll believe that this Assyrian
was actually like a wolf I must have some kind of proof;
Did he run on all fours and did he have a hairy tail and a big
red mouth and big white teeth and did he say Woof woof
woof?
Frankly I think it very unlikely, and all you were entitled to
say, at the very most,
Was that the Assyrian cohorts came down like a lot of
Assyrian cohorts about to destroy the Hebrew host.
But that wasn't fancy enough for Lord Byron, oh dear me,
no, he had to invent a lot of figures of speech and then
interpolate them,
With the result that whenever you mention Old Testament
soldiers to people they say Oh yes, they're the ones that a
lot of wolves dressed up in gold and purple ate them.
That's the kind of thing that's being done all the time by
poets, from Homer to Tennyson;
They're always comparing ladies to lilies and veal to veni-
son,
And they always say things like that the snow is a white
blanket after a winter storm.
Oh it is, is it, all right then, you sleep under a six-inch
blanket of snow and I'll sleep under a half-inch blanket of
unpoetical blanket material and we'll see which one keeps
warm,
And after that maybe you'll begin to comprehend dimly
What I mean by too much metaphor and simile.

OGDEN NASH

261

PORTRAITS

My Last Duchess

That's my last Duchess painted on the wall,
Looking as if she were alive. I call
That piece a wonder, now: Frà Pandolf's hands
Worked busily a day, and there she stands.
Will't please you sit and look at her? I said
"Frà Pandolf" by design, for never read
Strangers like you that pictured countenance,
The depth and passion of its earnest glance,
But to myself they turned (since none puts by
The curtain I have drawn for you, but I)
And seemed as they would ask me, if they durst,

How such a glance came there; so, not the first
Are you to turn and ask thus. Sir, 'twas not
Her husband's presence only, called that spot
Of joy into the Duchess' cheek: perhaps
Frà Pandolf chanced to say, "Her mantle laps
Over my Lady's wrist too much," or "Paint
Must never hope to reproduce the faint
Half-flush that dies along her throat"; such stuff
Was courtesy, she thought, and cause enough
For calling up that spot of joy. She had
A heart—how shall I say?—too soon made glad,
Too easily impressed; she liked whate'er
She looked on, and her looks went everywhere.
Sir, 'twas all one! My favor at her breast,
The dropping of the daylight in the West,
The bough of cherries some officious fool
Broke in the orchard for her, the white mule
She rode with round the terrace—all and each
Would draw from her alike the approving speech,
Or blush, at least. She thanked men,—good; but thanked
Somehow—I know not how—as if she ranked
My gift of a nine-hundred-years'-old name
With anybody's gift. Who'd stoop to blame
This sort of trifling? Even had you skill
In speech—(which I have not)—to make your will
Quite clear to such an one, and say, "Just this
Or that in you disgusts me; here you miss,

Or there exceed the mark"—and if she let
Herself be lessoned so, nor plainly set
Her wits to yours, forsooth, and made excuse,
—E'en then would be some stooping, and I choose
Never to stoop. Oh, sir, she smiled, no doubt,
Whene'er I passed her; but who passed without
Much the same smile? This grew; I gave commands;
Then all smiles stopped together. There she stands
As if alive. Will't please you rise? We'll meet
The company below, then. I repeat,
The Count your master's known munificence
Is ample warrant that no just pretence
Of mine for dowry will be disallowed;
Though his fair daughter's self, as I avowed
At starting, is my object. Nay, we'll go
Together down, sir! Notice Neptune, though,
Taming a sea-horse, thought a rarity,
Which Claus of Innsbruck cast in bronze for me!

ROBERT BROWNING

Gunga Din

You may talk o' gin and beer
When you're quartered safe out 'ere,
An' you're sent to penny-fights an' Aldershot it;
But when it comes to slaughter
You will do your work on water,
An' you'll lick the bloomin' boots of 'im that's got it.
Now in Injia's sunny clime,
Where I used to spend my time
A-servin' of 'Er Majesty the Queen,
Of all them blackfaced crew
The finest man I knew
Was our regimental bhisti, Gunga Din.
      He was "Din! Din! Din!
  "You limpin' lump o' brick-dust, Gunga Din!
     "Hi! Slippy *hitherao!*
     "Water, get it! *Panee lao,*
  "You squidgy-nosed old idol, Gunga Din."

The uniform 'e wore
Was nothin' much before,
An' rather less than 'arf o' that be'ind,
For a piece o' twisty rag
An' a goatskin water-bag
Was all the field-equipment 'e could find.
When the sweatin' troop-train lay
In a sidin' through the day,
Where the 'eat would make your bloomin' eyebrows crawl,
We shouted "Harry By!"
Till our throats were bricky-dry,
Then we wopped 'im 'cause 'e couldn't serve us all.
　　　　It was "Din! Din! Din!
　"You 'eathen, where the mischief 'ave you been?
　　　　"You put some *juldee* in it
　　　　"Or I'll *marrow* you this minute
　"If you don't fill up my helmet, Gunga Din!"

'E would dot an' carry one
Till the longest day was done;
An' 'e didn't seem to know the use o' fear.
If we charged or broke or cut,
You could bet your bloomin' nut,
'E'd be waitin' fifty paces right flank rear.
With 'is mussick on 'is back,
'E would skip with our attack,
An' watch us till the bugles made "Retire,"
An' for all 'is dirty 'ide
'E was white, clear white, inside
When 'e went to tend the wounded under fire!
      It was "Din! Din! Din!"
  With the bullets kickin' dust-spots on the green.
     When the cartridges ran out,
     You could hear the front-ranks shout,
  "Hi! ammunition-mules an' Gunga Din!"

I shan't forgit the night
When I dropped be'ind the fight
With a bullet where my belt-plate should 'a' been.
I was chokin' mad with thirst,
An' the man that spied me first
Was our good old grinnin', gruntin' Gunga Din.
'E lifted up my 'ead,
An' he plugged me where I bled,
An' 'e guv me 'arf-a-pint o' water green.
It was crawlin' and it stunk,
But of all the drinks I've drunk,
I'm gratefullest to one from Gunga Din.
    It was "Din! Din! Din!
"'Ere's a beggar with a bullet through 'is spleen;
    "'E's chawin' up the ground,
    "An' 'e's kickin' all around:
"For Gawd's sake git the water, Gunga Din!"

'E carried me away
To where a dooli lay,
An' a bullet come an' drilled the beggar clean.
'E put me safe inside,
An' just before 'e died,
"I 'ope you liked your drink," sez Gunga Din.
So I'll meet 'im later on
At the place where 'e is gone—
Where it's always double drill and no canteen.
'E'll be squattin' on the coals
Givin' drink to poor damned souls,
An' I'll get a swig in hell from Gunga Din!
　　　Yes, Din! Din! Din!
　You Lazarushian-leather Gunga Din!
　　　Though I've belted you and flayed you,
　　　By the livin' Gawd that made you,
　You're a better man than I am, Gunga Din!

RUDYARD KIPLING

Porphyria's Lover

The rain set early in to-night,
　The sullen wind was soon awake,
It tore the elm-tops down for spite,
　And did its worst to vex the lake:
　I listened with heart fit to break.
When glided in Porphyria: straight
　She shut the cold out and the storm,
And kneeled and made the cheerless grate
　Blaze up, and all the cottage warm;
　Which done, she rose and from her form
Withdrew the dripping cloak and shawl,
　And laid her soiled gloves by, untied
Her hat and let the damp hair fall,
　And, last, she sat down by my side
　And called me. When no voice replied,
She put my arm about her waist,
　And made her smooth white shoulder bare,
And, stooping, made my cheek lie there,
　And spread o'er all her yellow hair,
Murmuring how she loved me—she
　Too weak, for all her heart's endeavor,
To set its struggling passion free
　From pride, and vainer ties dissever,
　And give herself to me for ever.

But passion sometimes would prevail,
    Nor could to-night's gay feast restrain
A sudden thought of one so pale
    For love of her, and all in vain:
    So, she was come through wind and rain.
Be sure I looked up at her eyes
    Happy and proud: at last I knew
Porphyria worshipped me: surprise
    Made my heart swell, and still it grew
    While I debated what to do.
That moment she was mine, mine, fair,
    Perfectly pure and good: I found
A thing to do, and all her hair
    In one long yellow string I wound
    Three times her little throat around,
And strangled her. No pain felt she;
    I am quite sure she felt no pain.
As a shut bud that holds a bee,
    I warily oped her lids: again
    Laughed the blue eyes without a stain.
And I untightened next the tress
    About her neck: her cheeks once more
Blushed bright beneath my burning kiss:
    I propped her head up as before,
    Only, this time my shoulder bore

Her head, which droops upon it still:
   The smiling rosy little head,
So glad it has its utmost will,
   That all it scorned at once is fled,
   And I, its love, am gained instead!
Porphyria's love: she guessed not how
   Her darling one wish would be heard
And thus we sit together now,
   And all night long we have not stirred,
   And yet God has not said a word!

ROBERT BROWNING

La Belle Dame Sans Merci

O what can ail thee, knight-at-arms,
    Alone and palely loitering?
The sedge has wither'd from the lake,
    And no birds sing.

O what can ail thee, knight-at-arms,
    So haggard and so woe-begone?
The squirrel's granary is full,
    And the harvest's done.

I see a lily on thy brow
    With anguish moist and fever dew;
And on thy cheeks a fading rose
    Fast withereth too.

I met a lady in the meads,
    Full beautiful—a faëry's child,
Her hair was long, her foot was light,
    And her eyes were wild.

I made a garland for her head,
    And bracelets too, and fragrant zone;
She look'd at me as she did love,
    And made sweet moan.

I set her on my pacing steed,
   And nothing else saw all day long,
For sidelong would she bend, and sing
   A faëry's song.

She found me roots of relish sweet,
   And honey wild, and manna dew,
And sure in language strange she said,
   "I love thee true!"

She took me to her elfin grot,
   And there she wept and sigh'd full sore,
And there I shut her wild, wild eyes
   With kisses four.

And there she lulled me asleep,
   And there I dream'd,—ah! woe betide!
The latest dream I ever dream'd
   On the cold hill's side.

I saw pale kings and princes too,
   Pale warriors, death-pale were they all;
They cried—"La Belle Dame sans Merci
   Hath thee in thrall!"

I saw their starved lips in the gloam,
  With horrid warning gaped wide,
And I awoke and found me here,
  On the cold hill's side.

And this is why I sojourn here,
  Alone and palely loitering,
Though the sedge is wither'd from the lake,
  And no birds sing.

JOHN KEATS

Mr. Flood's Party

Old Eben Flood, climbing alone one night
Over the hill between the town below
And the forsaken upland hermitage
That held as much as he should ever know
On earth again of home, paused warily.
The road was his with not a native near;
And Eben, having leisure, said aloud,
For no man else in Tilbury Town to hear:

"Well, Mr. Flood, we have the harvest moon
Again, and we may not have many more;
The bird is on the wing, the poet says,
And you and I have said it here before.
Drink to the bird." He raised up to the light
The jug that he had gone so far to fill,
And answered huskily: "Well, Mr. Flood,
Since you propose it, I believe I will."

Alone, as if enduring to the end
A valiant armor of scarred hopes outworn,
He stood there in the middle of the road
Like Roland's ghost winding a silent horn.

Below him, in the town among the trees,
Where friends of other days had honored him,
A phantom salutation of the dead
Rang thinly till old Eben's eyes were dim.

Then, as a mother lays her sleeping child
Down tenderly, fearing it may awake,
He set the jug down slowly at his feet
With trembling care, knowing that most things break:
And only when assured that on firm earth
It stood, as the uncertain lives of men
Assuredly did not, he paced away,
And with his hand extended paused again:

"Well, Mr. Flood, we have not met like this
In a long time; and many a change has come
To both of us, I fear, since last it was
We had a drop together. Welcome home!"
Convivially returning with himself,
Again he raised the jug up to the light;
And with an acquiescent quaver said,
"Well, Mr. Flood, if you insist, I might.

"Only a very little, Mr. Flood—
For auld lang syne. No more, sir; that will do."
So, for the time, apparently it did,

And Eben evidently thought so too:
For soon amid the silver loneliness
Of night he lifted up his voice and sang,
Secure, with only two moons listening,
Until the whole harmonious landscape range—

"For auld lang syne." The eary throat gave out,
The last word wavered, and the song was done.
He raised again the jug regretfully
And shook his head, and was again alone.
There was not much that was ahead of him,
And there was nothing in the town below—
Where strangers would have shut the many doors
That many friends had opened long ago.

EDWIN ARLINGTON ROBINSON

The Unknown Citizen

(To Js/07/M 378 This Marble Monument Is Erected
by the State)

He was found by the Bureau of Statistics to be
One against whom there was no official complaint,
And all the reports on his conduct agree
That, in the modern sense of an old-fashioned word, he was
   a saint,
For in everything he did he served the Greater Community.
Except for the War till the day he retired
He worked in a factory and never got fired,
But satisfied his employers, Fudge Motors Inc.
Yet he wasn't a scab or odd in his views,
For his Union reports that he paid his dues,
(Our report on his Union shows it was sound)
And our Social Psychology workers found
That he was popular with his mates and liked a drink.
The Press are convinced that he bought a paper every day
And that his reactions to advertisements were normal in
   every way.
Policies taken out in his name prove that he was fully
   insured,
And his Health-card shows he was once in hospital but left
   it cured.

Both Producers Research and High-Grade Living declare
He was fully sensible to the advantages of the Installment
    Plan
And had everything necessary to the Modern Man,
A phonograph, a radio, a car and a frigidaire.
Our researchers into Public Opinion are content
That he held the proper opinions for the time of year;
When there was peace, he was for peace; when there was
    war, he went.
He was married and added five children to the population,
Which our Eugenist says was the right number for a parent
    of his generation,
And our teachers report that he never interfered with their
    education.
Was he free? Was he happy? The question is absurd:
Had anything been wrong, we should certainly have heard.

W. H. AUDEN

PRAYER

Mihi Adhaerere Deo Bonum Est (My Good Consists in Cleaving to God)

God be in my hede
And in my understandyng.
God be in myne eyes
And in my lokyng.
God be in my mouth
And in my speakyng.
God be in my harte
And in my thynkyng.
God be at mine ende
And at my departyng.

ANONYMOUS

Psalm 23

The Lord is my shepherd; I shall not want.

He maketh me to lie down in green pastures: he leadeth me beside the still waters.

He restoreth my soul: he leadeth me in the paths of righteousness for his name's sake.

Yea, though I walk through the valley of the shadow of death, I will fear no evil: for thou art with me; thy rod and thy staff they comfort me.

Thou preparest a table before me in the presence of mine enemies: thou anointest my head with oil; my cup runneth over.

Surely goodness and mercy shall follow me all the days of my life: and I will dwell in the house of the Lord for ever.

Hanukkah Hymn

Rock of Ages, let our song
Praise Thy saving power;
Thou, amidst the raging foes,
Wast our sheltering tower.
Furious, they assailed us,
But Thine arm availed us,
And Thy word
Broke their sword
When our own strength failed us.

Kindling new the holy lamps,
Priest approved in suffering,
Purified the nation's shrine,
Brought to God their offering.
And His courts surrounding,
Hear, in joy abounding,
Happy throngs
Singing songs
With a mighty sounding.

Children of the martyr race,
Whether free or fettered,
Wake the echoes of the songs
Where ye may be scattered.
Yours the message cheering
That the time is nearing
Which will see
All men free,
Tyrants disappearing.

ANONYMOUS

Prayer of St. Francis of Assisi

Lord, make me an instrument of your peace.
Where there is hatred, let me sow love;
Where there is injury, pardon;
Where there is doubt, faith;
Where there is despair, hope;
Where there is darkness, light;
And where there is sadness, joy.
O, Divine Master, grant that I may not so much seek to be
    consoled as to console;
To be understood as to understand;
To be loved as to love;
For it is in giving that we receive;
It is in pardoning that we are pardoned;
It is in dying that we are born to eternal life.

Prayer of an Unknown Confederate Soldier

I asked God for strength, that I might achieve,
I was made weak, that I might learn humbly to obey . . .
I asked for health, that I might do greater things,
I was given infirmity, that I might do better things . . .
I asked for riches, that I might be happy,
I was given poverty that I might be wise . . .
I asked for power, that I might have the praise of men,
I was given weakness, that I might feel the need of God . . .
I asked for all things, that I might enjoy life,
I was given life, that I might enjoy all things . . .
I got nothing that I asked for—but everything that I had
  hoped for.
Almost despite myself, my unspoiled prayers were ans-
  wered.
I am among all men, most richly blessed.

Bless This House

Bless this house, O Lord, we pray
Make it safe by night and day:
Bless these walls so firm and stout
Keeping want and trouble out;

Bless the roof and chimneys tall,
Let Thy peace lie over all:
Bless this door, that it may prove
Ever open to joy and love.

Bless these windows shining bright,
Letting in God's heavenly light:
Bless the hearth ablazing there,
With smoke ascending like a prayer:

Bless the people here within,
Keep them pure and free from sin;
Bless us all that we may be
Fit, O Lord, to dwell with thee.

MARY H. BRAHE and HELEN TAYLOR

An Irish Wish

May the road rise to meet you.
May the wind be ever at your back.
May the Good Lord keep you in the hollow of His hand.
May your heart be as warm as your hearthstone.
And when you come to die may the wail of the poor be the
    only sorrow you'll leave behind.
May God bless you always.

ANONYMOUS

My Prayer

Great God, I ask thee for no meaner pelf
Than that I may not disappoint myself;
That in my action I may soar as high
As I can now discern with this clear eye.

And next in value, which thy kindness lends,
That I may greatly disappoint my friends,
Howe'er they think or hope that it may be,
They may not dream how thou'st distinguished me;

That my weak hand may equal my firm faith,
And my life practice more than my tongue saith;
  That my low conduct may not show,
    Nor my relenting lines,
  That I thy purpose did not know,
    Or overrated thy designs.

HENRY DAVID THOREAU

REBELLION

Dirge Without Music

I am not resigned to the shutting away of loving hearts in
    the hard ground.
So it is, and so it will be, for so it has been, time out of mind:
Into the darkness they go, the wise and the lovely.
    Crowned with lilies and with laurel they go; but I am
    not resigned.

Lovers and thinkers, into the earth with you.
Be one with the dull, the indiscriminate dust.
A fragment of what you felt, of what you knew,
A formula, a phrase remains,—but the best is lost.

The answers quick and keen, the honest look, the laughter, the love,—
They are gone. They are gone to feed the roses. Elegant and curled
Is the blossom. Fragrant is the blossom. I know. But I do not approve.
More precious was the light in your eyes than all the roses of the world.

Down, down, down into the darkness of the grave
Gently they go, the beautiful, the tender, the kind;
Quietly they go, the intelligent, the witty, the brave.
I know. But I do not approve. And I am not resigned.

EDNA ST. VINCENT MILLAY

Do Not Go Gentle into That Good Night

Do not go gentle into that good night,
Old age should burn and rave at close of day;
Rage, rage against the dying of the light.

Though wise men at their end know dark is right,
Because their words had forked no lightning they
Do not go gentle into that good night.

Good men, the last wave by, crying how bright
Their frail deeds might have danced in a green bay,
Rage, rage against the dying of the light.

Wild men who caught and sang the sun in flight,
And learn, too late, they grieved it on its way,
Do not go gentle into that good night.

Grave men, near death, who see with blinding sight
Blind eyes could blaze like meteors and be gay,
Rage, rage against the dying of the light.

And you, my father, there on the sad height,
Curse, bless, me now with your fierce tears, I pray.
Do not go gentle into that good night.
Rage, rage against the dying of the light.

DYLAN THOMAS

REGRET

A Superscription

Look in my face; my name is Might-have-been;
I am also called No-more, Too-late, Farewell;
Unto thine ear I hold the dead-sea-shell
Cast up thy Life's foam-fretted feet between;
Unto thine eyes the glass where that is seen
Which had Life's form and Love's, but by my spell
Is now a shaken shadow intolerable,
Of ultimate things unuttered the frail screen.
Mark me, how still I am! But should there dart
One moment through thy soul the soft surprise
Of that winged Peace which lulls the breath of sighs,—
Then shalt thou see me smile, and turn apart
Thy visage to mine ambush at thy heart
Sleepless with cold commemorative eyes.

DANTE GABRIEL ROSSETTI

Ah, Fading Joy

Ah, fading joy, how quickly art thou past!
   Yet we thy ruine haste:
As if the cares of Humane Life were few,
   We seek out new,
And follow Fate that does too fast pursue.

See how on ev'ry Bough the Birds express
   In their sweet notes their happiness.
   They all enjoy and nothing spare;
But on their Mother Nature lay their care;
Why then should Man, the Lord of all below,
   Such troubles chuse to know,
As none of all his Subjects undergo?

JOHN DRYDEN

Broken Friendship

Alas! they had been friends in youth,
But whispering tongues can poison truth!
And constancy lives in realms above!
And life is thorny, and Youth is vain!
And to be wroth with one we love,
Doth work like madness in the brain!
They parted—ne'er to meet again!
But never either found another
To free the hollow heart from paining!
They stood aloof, the scars remaining;
Like cliffs which had been rent asunder!
A dreary sea now flows between;
But neither heat, nor frost, nor thunder,
Shall wholly do away, I ween,
The marks of that which once had been.

SAMUEL TAYLOR COLERIDGE

My Playmate

The pines were dark on Ramoth hill,
  Their song was soft and low;
The blossoms in the sweet May wind
  Were falling like the snow.

The blossoms drifted at our feet,
  The orchard birds sang clear;
The sweetest and the saddest day
  It seemed of all the year.

For, more to me than birds or flowers,
  My playmate left her home.
And took with her the laughing spring,
  The music and the bloom.

She kissed the lips of kith and kin,
  She laid her hand in mine:
What more could ask the bashful boy
  Who fed her father's kine?

She left us in the bloom of May:
  The constant years told o'er
Their seasons with as sweet May morns,
  But she came back no more.

I walk, with noiseless feet, the round
   Of uneventful years;
Still o'er and o'er I sow the spring
   And reap the autumn ears.

She lives where all the golden year
   Her summer roses blow;
The dusky children of the sun
   Before her come and go.

There haply with her jewelled hands
   She smooths her silken gown,—
No more the homespun lap wherein
   I shook the walnuts down.

The wild grapes wait us by the brook,
   The brown nuts on the hill,
And still the May-day flowers make sweet
   The woods of Follymill.

The lilies blossom in the pond,
   The bird builds in the tree,
The dark pines sing on Ramoth hill
   The slow song of the sea.

I wonder if she thinks of them,
   And how the old time seems,—
If ever the pines of Ramoth wood
   Are sounding in her dreams.

I see her face, I hear her voice;
  Does she remember mine?
And what to her is now the boy
  Who fed her father's kine?

What cares she that the orioles build
  For other eyes than ours,—
That other hands with nuts are filled,
  And other laps with flowers?

O playmate in the golden time!
  Our mossy seat is green,
Its fringing violets blossom yet,
  The old trees o'er it lean.

The winds so sweet with birch and fern
  A sweeter memory blow;
And there in spring the veeries sing
  The song of long ago.

And still the pines of Ramoth wood
  Are moaning like the sea,—
The moaning of the sea of change
  Between myself and thee!

JOHN GREENLEAF WHITTIER

Lost Days

The lost days of my life until to-day,
   What were they, could I see them on the street
   Lie as they fell? Would they be ears of wheat
Sown once for food but trodden into clay?
Or golden coins squandered and still to pay?
   Or drops of blood dabbling the guilty feet?
   Or such spilt water as in dreams must cheat
The undying throats of Hell, athirst alway?

I do not see them here; but after death
   God knows I know the faces I shall see
Each one a murdered self, with low last breath.
   'I am thyself,—what hast thou done to me?'
'And I—and I—thyself,' (lo! each one saith,)
   'And thou thyself to all eternity!'

DANTE GABRIEL ROSSETTI

Maud Muller

Maud Muller on a summer's day
Raked the meadow sweet with hay.

Beneath her torn hat glowed the wealth
Of simple beauty and rustic health.

Singing, she wrought, and her merry glee
The mock-bird echoed from his tree.

But when she glanced to the far-off town,
White from its hill-slope looking down,

The sweet song died, and a vague unrest
And a nameless longing filled her breast,—

A wish that she hardly dared to own,
For something better than she had known.

The Judge rode slowly down the lane,
Smoothing his horse's chestnut mane.

He drew his bridle in the shade
Of the apple-trees, to greet the maid,

And asked a draught from the spring that flowed
Through the meadow across the road.

She stooped where the cool spring bubbled up,
And filled for him her small tin cup,

And blushed as she gave it, looking down
On her feet so bare, and her tattered gown.

"Thanks!" said the Judge, "a sweeter draught
From a fairer hand was never quaffed."

He spoke of the grass and flowers and trees,
Of the singing birds and the humming bees;

Then talked of the haying, and wondered whether
The cloud in the west would bring foul weather.

And Maud forgot her brier-torn gown,
And her graceful ankles bare and brown;

And listened, while a pleased surprise
Looked from her long-lashed hazel eyes.

At last, like one who for delay
Seeks a vain excuse, he rode away.

Maud Muller looked and sighed: "Ah me!
That I the Judge's bride might be!

"He would dress me up in silks so fine,
And praise and toast me at his wine.

"My father should wear a broadcloth coat,
My brother should sail a painted boat.

"I'd dress my mother so grand and gay,
And the baby should have a new toy each day.

"And I'd feed the hungry and clothe the poor,
And all should bless me who left our door."

The Judge looked back as he climbed the hill,
And saw Maud Muller standing still.

"A form more fair, a face more sweet,
Ne'er hath it been my lot to meet.

"And her modest answer and graceful air
Show her wise and good as she is fair.

"Would she were mine, and I to-day,
Like her, a harvester of hay;

"No doubtful balance of rights and wrongs,
Nor weary lawyers with endless tongues,

"But low of cattle and song of birds,
And health and quiet and loving words."

But he thought of his sisters, proud and cold,
And his mother, vain of her rank and gold.

So, closing his heart, the Judge rode on,
And Maud was left in the field alone.

But the lawyers smiled that afternoon,
When he hummed in court an old love-tune;

And the young girl mused beside the well
Till the rain on the unraked clover fell.

He wedded a wife of richest dower,
Who lived for fashion, as he for power.

Yet oft, in his marble hearth's bright glow,
He watched a picture come and go;

And sweet Maud Muller's hazel eyes
Looked out in their innocent surprise.

Oft, when the wine in his glass was red,
He longed for the wayside well instead;

And closed his eyes on his garnished rooms
To dream of meadows and clover-blooms.

And the proud man sighed, with a secret pain,
"Ah, that I were free again!

"Free as when I rode that day,
Where the barefoot maiden raked her hay."

She wedded a man unlearned and poor,
And many children played round her door.

But care and sorrow, and childbirth pain,
Left their traces on heart and brain.

And oft, when the summer sun shone hot
On the new-mown hay in the meadow lot,

And she heard the little spring brook fall
Over the roadside, through the wall,

In the shade of the apple-tree again
She saw a rider draw his rein;

And, gazing down with timid grace,
She felt his pleased eyes read her face.

Sometimes her narrow kitchen walls
Stretched away into stately halls;

The weary wheel to a spinet turned,
The tallow candle an astral burned,

And for him who sat by the chimney lug,
Dozing and grumbling o'er pipe and mug,

A manly form at her side she saw,
And joy was duty and love was law.

Then she took up her burden of life again
Saying only, "It might have been."

Alas for maiden, alas for Judge,
For rich repiner and household drudge!

God pity them both! and pity us all,
Who vainly the dreams of youth recall.

For of all sad words of tongue or pen,
The saddest are these: "It might have been!"

Ah, well! for us all some sweet hope lies
Deeply buried from human eyes;

And, in the hereafter, angels may
Roll the stone from its grave away!

JOHN GREENLEAF WHITTIER

Who Would Have Thought?

Who would have thought my shrivelled heart
Could have recovered greenness? It was gone
   Quite under ground, as flowers depart
To feed their mother-root when they have blown;
     Where they together
     All the hard weather,
Dead to the world, keep house unkown.

Dead are thy wonders, Lord of Power,
Killing and quickening, bringing down to hell
   And up to heaven in an hour;
Making a chiming of a passing bell.
     We say amiss,
     This or that is:
Thy word is all, if we could spell.

And now in age I bud again;
After so many deaths I live and write;
I once more smell the dew and rain,
And relish versing: O my only Light,
    It cannot be
    That I am he
On whom thy tempest fell all night.

GEORGE HERBERT

Evolution

Out of the dusk a shadow,
Then, a spark;
Out of the cloud a silence,
Then, a lark;
Out of the heart a rapture,
Then, a pain;
Out of the dead, cold ashes,
Life again.

JOHN BANISTER TABB

I Am a Parcel of Vain Strivings Tied

I am a parcel of vain strivings tied
    By a chance bond together,
  Dangling this way and that, their links
    Were made so loose and wide,
        Methinks,
      For milder weather.

A bunch of violets without their roots,
    And sorrel intermixed,
  Encircled by a wisp of straw
    Once coiled about their shoots,
      The law
      By which I'm fixed.

A nosegay which Time clutched from out
    Those fair Elysian fields,
  With weeds and broken stems, in haste,
    Doth make the rabble rout
      That waste
      The day he yields.

And here I bloom for a short hour unseen,
Drinking my juices up,
With no root in the land
To keep my branches green,
But stand
In a bare cup.

Some tender buds were left upon my stem
In mimicry of life,
But ah! the children will not know.
Till time has withered them,
The woe
With which they're rife.

But now I see I was not plucked for naught,
And after in life's vase
Of glass set while I might survive,
But by a kind hand brought
Alive
To a strange place.

That stock thus thinned will soon redeem its hours,
And by another year,
Such as God knows, with freer air,
More fruits and fairer flowers
Will bear,
While I droop here.

HENRY DAVID THOREAU

A Death Blow Is a Life Blow

A Death blow is a Life blow to Some
Who till they died, did not alive become—
Who had they lived, had died but when
They died, Vitality begun.

EMILY DICKINSON

I Thank You God

i thank You God for most this amazing
day:for the leaping greenly spirits of trees
and a blue true dream of sky;and for everything
which is natural which is infinite which is yes

(i who have died am alive again today,
and this is the sun's birthday;this is the birth
day of life and of love and wings:and of the day
great happening illimitably earth)

how should tasting touching hearing seeing
breathing any—lifted from the no
of all nothing—human merely being
doubt unimaginable You?

(now the ears of my ears awake and
now the eyes of my eyes are opened)

e. e. cummings

Shadows

And if tonight my soul may find her peace in sleep, and sink
    in good oblivion,
and in the morning wake like a newly opened flower
then I have been dipped again in God, and new-created.
And if, as weeks go round, in the dark of the moon
my spirit darkens and goes out, and soft strange gloom
pervades my movements and my thoughts and words
then I shall know that I am walking still
with God, we are close together now the moon's in shadow,

And if, as autumn deepens and darkens
I feel the pain of falling leaves, and stems that break in
    storms
and trouble and dissolution and distress
and then the softness of deep shadows folding, folding
around my soul and spirit, around my lips
so sweet, like a swoon, or more like the drowse of a low, sad
    song
singing darker than the nightingale, on, on to the solstice
and the silence of short days, the silence of the year, the
    shadow,
then I shall know that my life is moving still
with the dark earth, and drenched
with the deep oblivion of earth's lapse and renewal.

And if, in the changing phases of man's life
I fall in sickness and in misery
my wrists seem broken and my heart seems dead
and strength is gone, and my life
is only the leavings of a life:
and still, among it all, snatches of lovely oblivion, and
    snatches of renewal
odd, wintry flowers upon the withered stem, yet new,
    strange flowers
such as my life has not brought forth before, new blossoms
    of me—

then I must know that still
I am in the hands of the unknown God,
he is breaking me down to his own oblivion
to send me forth on a new morning, a new man.

D. H. LAWRENCE

Hertha

I am that which began;
   Out of me the years roll;
Out of me God and man;
   I am equal and whole;
God changes, and man, and the form of them bodily; I am
   the soul.

Before ever land was,
   Before ever the sea,
Or soft hair of the grass,
   Or fair limbs of the tree,
Or the flesh-coloured fruit of my branches, I was, and thy
   soul was in me.

First life on my sources
   First drifted and swam;
Out of me are the forces
   That save it or damn;
Out of me man and woman, and wild-beast and bird; before
   God was, I am.

Beside or above me
　　Nought is there to go;
Love or unlove me,
　　Unknow me or know,
I am that which unloves me and loves; I am stricken, and I
　　am the blow.

I the mark that is missed
　　And the arrows that miss,
I the mouth that is kissed
　　And the breath in the kiss,
The search, and the sought, and the seeker, the soul and
　　the body that is.

I am that thing which blesses
　　My spirit elate;
That which caresses
　　With hands uncreate.
My limbs unbegotten that measure the length of the meas-
　　ure of fate.

But what thing dost thou now,
　　Looking Godward, to cry
'I am I, thou art thou,
　　I am low, thou art high'?
I am thou, whom thou seekest to find him; find thou but
　　thyself, thou art I.

I the grain and the furrow,
   The plough-cloven clod
And the ploughshare drawn thorough,
Hast thou known how I fashioned thee,
   Child, underground?
Fire that impassioned thee,
   Iron that bound,
Dim changes of water, what thing of all these hast thou
   known of or found?

Canst thou say in thine heart
   Thou hast seen with thine eyes
With what cunning of art
   Thou wast wrought in what wise,
By what force of what stuff thou wast shapen, and shown
   on my breast to the skies?

Who hath given, who hath sold it thee,
   Knowledge of me?
Hath the wilderness told it thee?
   Hast thou learnt of the sea?
Hast thou communed in spirit with night? have the winds
   taken counsel with thee?

Have I set such a star
    To show light on thy brow
That thou sawest from afar
    What I show to thee now?
Have ye spoken as brethren together, the sun and the
    mountains and thou?

What is here, dost thou know it?
    What was, hast thou known?
Prophet nor poet
    Nor tripod nor throne
Nor spirit nor flesh can make answer, but only thy mother
    alone.

Mother, not maker,
    Born, and not made;
Though her children forsake her,
    Allured or afraid,
Praying prayers to the God of their fashion, she stirs not
    for all that have prayed.

A creed is a rod,
To grow straight in the strength of thy spirit, and live out
    thy life as the light.

I am in thee to save thee,
    As my soul in thee saith;
Give thou as I gave thee,
    Thy life-blood and breath,
Green leaves of thy labour, white flowers of thy thought,
    and red fruit of thy death.

Be the ways of thy giving
    As mine were to thee;
The free life of thy living,
    Be the gift of it free;
Not as servant to lord, nor as master to slave, shalt thou
    give thee to me.

O children of banishment,
    Souls overcast,
Were the lights ye see vanish meant
    Alway to last,
Ye would know not the sun overshining the shadows and
    stars overpast.

I that saw where ye trod
    The dim paths of the night
Set the shadow called God
    In your skies to give light;
But the morning of manhood is risen, and the shadowless
    soul is in sight.

The tree many-rooted
That swells to the sky
With frondage red-fruited,
The life-tree am I;
In the buds of your lives is the sap of my leaves: ye shall live
and not die.

But the Gods of your fashion
That take and that give,
In their pity and passion
That scourge and forgive,
That are worms that are bred in the bark that falls off; they
shall die and not live.

My own blood is what stanches
The wounds in my bark;
Stars caught in my branches
Make day of the dark,
And are worshiped as suns till the sunrise shall tread out
their fires as a spark.

Where dead ages hide under
The live roots of the tree,
In my darkness the thunder
Makes utterance of me;
In the clash of my boughs with each other ye hear the
waves sound of the sea.

That noise is of Time,
    As his feathers are spread
And his feet set to climb
    Through the boughs overhead,
And my foliage rings round him and rustles, and branches
    are bent with his tread.

The storm-winds of ages
    Blow through me and cease,
The war-wind that rages,
    The spring-wind of peace,
Ere the breath of them roughens my tresses, ere one of my
    blossoms increase.

All sounds of all changes,
    All shadows and lights
On the world's mountain-ranges
    And stream-riven heights,
Whose tongue is the wind's tongue and language of storm-
    clouds or earth-shaking nights;

All forms of all faces,
    All works of all hands
In unsearchable places
    Of time-stricken lands,
All death and all life, and all reigns and all ruins, drop
    through me as sands

Though sore be my burden
    And more than ye know,
And my growth have no guerdon
    But only to grow,
Yet I fail not of growing for lightnings above me or death-
    worms below.

These too have their part in me,
    As I too in these;
Such fire is at heart in me,
    Such sap is this tree's,
Which hath in it all sounds and all secrets of infinite lands
    and of seas.

In the spring-coloured hours
    When my mind was as May's,
There brake forth of me flowers
    By centuries of days,
Strong blossoms with perfume of manhood, shot out from
    my spirit as rays.

And the sound of them springing
    And smell of their shoots
Were as warmth and sweet singing
    And strength to my roots;
And the lives of my children made perfect with freedom of
    soul were my fruits.

I bid you but be;
  I have need not of prayer;
I have need of you free
  As your mouths of mine air;
That my heart may be greater within me, beholding the
  fruits of me fair.

More fair than strange fruit is
  Of faiths ye espouse;
In me only the root is
  That blooms in your boughs;
Behold now your God that ye made you, to feed him with
  faith of your vows.

In the darkening and whitening
  Abysses adored,
With dayspring and lightning
  For lamp and for sword,
God thunders in heaven, and his angels are red with the
  wrath of the Lord.

O my sons, O too dutiful
  Toward Gods not of me,
Was not I enough beautiful?
  Was it hard to be free?
For behold, I am with you, am in you and of you; look forth
  now and see.

Lo, winged with world's wonders,
  With miracles shod,
With the fires of his thunders
  For raiment and rod,
God trembles in heaven, and his angels are white with the
  terror of God.

For his twilight is come on him,
  His anguish is here;
And his spirits gaze dumb on him,
  Grown grey from his fear;
And his hour taketh hold on him striken, the last of his
  infinite year.

Thought made him and breaks him,
  Truth slays and forgives;
But to you, as time takes him,
  This new thing it gives,
Even love, the beloved Republic, that feeds upon freedom
  and lives.

For truth only is living,
  Truth only is whole,
And the love of his giving
  Man's polestar and pole;
Man, pulse of my centre, and fruit of my body, and seed of
  my soul.

One birth of my bosom;
  One beam of mine eye;
One topmost blossom
  That scales the sky;
Man, equal and one with me, man that is made of me, man
  that is I.

ALGERNON CHARLES SWINBURNE

ROMANCE

How Do I Love Thee?

How do I love thee? Let me count the ways.
I love thee to the depth and breadth and height
My soul can reach, when feeling out of sight
For the ends of Being and ideal Grace.
I love thee to the level of everyday's
Most quiet need, by sun and candle-light.
I love thee freely, as men strive for Right;
I love thee purely, as they turn from Praise.
I love thee with the passion put to use
In my old griefs, and with my childhood's faith.
I love thee with a love I seemed to lose
With my lost saints,—I love thee with the breath,
Smiles, tears, of all my life!—and, if God choose,
I shall but love thee better after death.

ELIZABETH BARRETT BROWNING

The Legacy

When last I died, and, dear, I die
  As often as from thee I go,
  Though it be but an hour ago
—And lovers' hours be full eternity—
I can remember yet, that I
  Something did say, and something did bestow;
Though I be dead, which sent me, I might be
Mine own executor, and legacy.

I heard me say, "Tell her anon,
  That myself," that is you, not I,
  "Did kill me," and when I felt me die,
I bid me send my heart, when I was gone;
But I alas! could there find none;
  When I had ripp'd, and search'd where hearts should be
It kill'd me again, that I who still was true
In life, in my last will should cozen you.

Yet I found something like a heart,
   But colors it and corners had;
   It was not good, it was not bad,
It was entire to none, and few had part;
As good as could be made by art
   It seemed, and therefore for our loss be sad.
I meant to send that heart instead of mine,
But O! no man could hold it, for 'twas thine.

JOHN DONNE

When Our Two Souls Stand Up

When our two souls stand up erect and strong,
Face to face, silent, drawing nigh and nigher,
Until the lengthening wings break into fire
At either curvéd point,—what bitter wrong
Can the earth do to us, that we should not long
Be here contented? Think. In mounting higher,
The angels would press on us and aspire
To drop some golden orb of perfect song
Into our deep, dear silence. Let us stay
Rather on earth, Belovéd,—where the unfit
Contrarious moods of men recoil away
And isolate pure spirits, and permit
A place to stand and love in for a day,
With darkness and the death-hour rounding it.

ELIZABETH BARRETT BROWNING

To ——

One word is too often profaned
　　For me to profane it,
One feeling too falsely disdained
　　For thee to disdain it;
One hope is too like despair
　　For prudence to smother,
And pity from thee more dear
　　Than that from another.

I can give not what men call love,
　　But wilt thou accept not
The worship the heart lifts above
　　And the heavens reject not,—
The desire of the moth for the star,
　　Of the night for the morrow,
The devotion to something afar
　　From the sphere of our sorrow?

PERCY BYSSHE SHELLEY

To Celia

Drink to me only with thine eyes,
   And I will pledge with mine;
Or leave a kiss but in the cup
   And I'll not look for wine.
The thirst that from the soul doth rise
   Doth ask a drink divine;
But might I of Jove's nectar sup,
   I would not change for thine.

I sent thee late a rosy wreath,
   Not so much honoring thee
As giving it a hope that there
   It could not withered be;
But thou thereon didst only breathe
   And sent'st it back to me;
Since when it grows, and smells, I swear,
   Not of itself but thee!

BEN JONSON

The Passionate Shepherd to His Love

Come live with me and be my love,
And we will all the pleasures prove
That hills and valleys, dales and fields,
And all the craggy mountains yields.

And we will sit upon the rocks
Seeing the shepherds feed their flocks,
By shallow rivers, to whose falls
Melodious birds sing madrigals.

And I will make thee beds of roses
And a thousand fragrant posies,
A cap of flowers, and a kirtle
Embroidered all with leaves of myrtle;

A gown made of the finest wool,
Which from our pretty lambs we pull;
Fair linéd slippers for the cold,
With buckles of the purest gold;

A belt of straw and ivy buds
With coral clasps and amber studs:
And if these pleasures may thee move,
Come live with me and be my love.

The shepherd swains shall dance and sing
For thy delight each May morning;
If these delights thy mind may move,
Then live with me and be my love.

CHRISTOPHER MARLOWE

Because

Because you come to me with naught save love,
And hold my hand and lift mine eyes above,
A wider world of hope and joy I see,
Because you come to me.

Because you speak to me in accents sweet,
I find the roses waking round my feet,
And I am led through tears of joy to see,
Because you speak to me.

Because God made thee mine I'll cherish thee
Through light and darkness, through all time to be,
And pray His love may make our lives divine.
Because God made thee mine.

EDWARD TESCHEMACHER

To Althea, from Prison

When Love with unconfinèd wings
   Hovers within my gates,
And my divine Althea brings
   To whisper at the grates;
When I lie tangled in her hair
   And fettered to her eye,
The birds that wanton in the air
   Know no such liberty.

When flowing cups run swiftly round
   With no allaying Thames,
Our careless heads with roses bound,
   Our hearts with loyal flames;
When thirsty grief in wine we steep,
   When healths and draughts go free,
Fishes that tipple in the deep
   Know no such liberty.

When, like committed linnets, I
    With shriller throat will sing
The sweetness, mercy, majesty,
    And glories of my king;
When I shall voice aloud how good
    He is, how great should be,
Enlargèd winds, that curl the flood,
    Know no such liberty.

Stone walls do not a prison make,
    Nor iron bars a cage;
Minds innocent and quiet take
    That for an hermitage;
If I have freedom in my love
    And in my soul am free,
Angels alone, that soar above,
    Enjoy such liberty.

RICHARD LOVELACE

Bedouin Song

From the Desert I come to thee
  On a stallion shod with fire;
And the winds are left behind
  In the speed of my desire.
Under thy window I stand,
  And the midnight hears my cry:
I love thee, I love but thee,
  With a love that shall not die
    Till the sun grows cold,
    And the stars are old,
    And the leaves of the Judgment Book unfold!

Look from thy window and see
  My passion and my pain;
I lie on the sands below,
  And I faint in thy disdain.
Let the night-winds touch thy brow
  With the heat of my burning sigh,
And melt thee to hear the vow
  Of a love that shall not die
    Till the sun grows cold,
    And the stars are old,
    And the leaves of the Judgment Book unfold!

My steps are nightly driven,
   By the fever in my breast,
To hear from thy lattice breathed
   The word that shall give me rest.
Open the door of thy heart,
   And open thy chamber door,
And my kisses shall teach thy lips
   The love that shall fade no more
      Till the sun grows cold,
      And the stars are old,
      And the leaves of the Judgment Book unfold!

BAYARD TAYLOR

The Taxi

When I go away from you
The world beats dead
Like a slackened drum.
I call out for you against the jutted stars
And shout into the ridges of the wind.
Streets coming fast,
One after the other,
Wedge you away from me,
And the lamps of the city prick my eyes
So that I can no longer see your face.
Why should I leave you,
To wound myself upon the sharp edges of the night?

AMY LOWELL

Somewhere I Have Never Travelled

somewhere i have never travelled,gladly beyond
any experience,your eyes have their silence:
in your most frail gesture are things which enclose me,
or which i cannot touch because they are too near

your slightest look easily will unclose me
though i have closed myself as fingers,
you open always petal by petal myself as Spring opens
(touching skilfully,mysteriously)her first rose

or if your wish be to close me,i and
my life will shut very beautifully,suddenly,
as when the heart of this flower imagines
the snow carefully everywhere descending;

nothing which we are to perceive in this world equals
the power of your intense fragility:whose texture
compels me with the color of its countries,
rendering death and forever with each breathing

(i do not know what it is about you that closes
and opens;only something in me understands
the voice of your eyes is deeper than all roses)
nobody,not even the rain,has such small hands

e. e. cummings

A Match

If love were what the rose is,
  And I were like the leaf,
Our lives would grow together
In sad or singing weather,
Blown fields or flowerful closes,
  Green pleasure or gray grief;
If love were what the rose is,
  And I were like the leaf.

If I were what the words are,
  And love were like the tune,
With double sound and single
Delight our lips would mingle,
With kisses glad as birds are
  That get sweet rain at noon;
If I were what the words are,
  And love were like the tune.

If you were life, my darling,
   And I your love were death,
We'd shine and snow together
Ere March made sweet the weather
With daffodil and starling
   And hours of fruitful breath;
If you were life, my darling,
   And I your love were death.

If you were thrall to sorrow,
   And I were page to joy,
We'd play for lives and seasons
With loving looks and treasons
And tears of night and morrow
   And laughs of maid and boy;
If you were thrall to sorrow,
   And I were page to joy.

If you were April's lady,
   And I were lord in May,
We'd throw with leaves for hours
And draw for days with flowers,
Till day like night were shady
   And night were bright like day;
If you were April's lady,
   And I were lord in May.

If you were queen of pleasure,
  And I were king of pain,
We'd hunt down love together,
Pluck out his flying feather,
And teach his feet a measure,
  And find his mouth a rein;
If you were queen of pleasure,
  And I were king of pain.

ALGERNON CHARLES SWINBURNE

SACRIFICES

She Rose to His Requirement

She rose to His Requirement—dropt
The Playthings of Her Life
To take the honorable Work
Of Woman, and of Wife—

If ought She missed in Her new Day,
Of Amplitude, or Awe—
Or first Prospective—Or the Gold
In using, wear away,

It lay unmentioned—as the Sea
Develop Pearl, and Weed,
But only to Himself—be known
The Fathoms they abide—

EMILY DICKINSON

To Primroses
Filled with Morning Dew.

Why do ye weep, sweet babes? Can tears
Speak grief in you,
Who were but born
Just as the modest morn
Teemed her refreshing dew?
Alas! ye have not known that shower
That mars a flower:
Nor felt the unkind
Breath of a blasting wind;
Nor are ye worn with years;
Or warped as we,
Who think it strange to see
Such pretty flowers, like to orphans young.
Speaking by tears before ye have a tongue.

Speak, whimpering younglings, and make known
The reason why
Ye droop and weep.
Is it for want of sleep,
Or childish lullaby?
Or that ye have not seen as yet
The violet?

Or brought a kiss
From that sweetheart to this?
No, no; this sorrow shown
By your tears shed,
Would have this lecture read:
That things of greatest, so of meanest worth,
Conceived with grief are, and with tears brought forth.

ROBERT HERRICK

Eros Turannos

She fears him, and will always ask
   What fated her to choose him;
She meets in his engaging mask
   All reasons to refuse him;
But what she meets and what she fears
Are less than are the downward years,
Drawn slowly to the foamless weirs
   Of age, were she to lose him.

Between a blurred sagacity
   That once had power to sound him,
And Love, that will not let him be
   The Judas that she found him,
Her pride assuages her almost,
As if it were alone the cost,—
He sees that he will not be lost,
   And waits and looks around him.

A sense of ocean and old trees
   Envelops and allures him;
Tradition, touching all he sees,
   Beguiles and reassures him;
And all her doubts of what he says
Are dimmed with what she knows of days—
Till even prejudice delays
   And fades, and she secures him.

The falling leaf inaugurates
   The reign of her confusion;
The pounding wave reverberates
   The dirge of her illusion;
And home, where passion lived and died,
Becomes a place where she can hide,
While all the town and harbor side
   Vibrate with her seclusion.

We tell you, tapping on our brows,
   The story as it should be,—
As if the story of a house
   Were told, or ever could be;
We'll have no kindly veil between
Her visions and those we have seen,—
As if we guessed what hers have been,
   Or what they are or would be.

Meanwhile we do no harm; for they
   That with a god have striven,
Not hearing much of what we say,
   Take what the god has given;
Though like waves breaking it may be
Or like a changed familiar tree,
Or like a stairway to the sea
   Where down the blind are driven.

EDWIN ARLINGTON ROBINSON

SOUL

Darest Thou Now O Soul

Darest thou now O soul,
Walk out with me toward the unknown region,
Where neither ground is for the feet nor any path to
  follow?

No map there, nor guide,
Nor voice sounding, nor touch of human hand,
Nor face with blooming flesh, nor lips, nor eyes, are in that
  land.

I know it not O soul,
Nor dost thou, all is a blank before us,
All waits undream'd of in that region, that inaccessible land.

Till when the ties loosen,
All but the ties eternal, Time and Space,
Nor darkness, gravitation sense, nor any bounds
   bounding us.

Then we burst forth, we float,
In Time and Space O soul, prepared for them,
Equal, equipt at last (O joy! O fruit of all!) them to fulfill
   O soul.

WALT WHITMAN

I Sought My Soul

I sought my soul,
  But my soul I could not see.
I sought my God,
  But my God eluded me.
I sought my brother,
  And I found all three.

ANONYMOUS

The Old Stoic

Riches I hold in light esteem,
And love I laugh to scorn;
And lust of fame was but a dream,
That vanished with the morn;

And if I pray, the only prayer
That moves my lips for me
Is, "Leave the heart that now I bear,
And give me liberty!"

Yes, as my swift days near the goal,
'Tis all that I implore;
In life and death a chainless soul,
With courage to endure.

EMILY BRONTË

To the Soul

Dull soul aspire;
Thou art not earth. Mount higher!
Heaven gave the spark; to it return the fire.

Let sin ne'er quench
Thy high-flamed spirit hence;
To earth the heat, to heaven the flame dispense!

Rejoice! Rejoice!
Turn, turn, each part a voice;
While to the heart-strings' tune ye all rejoice.

The house is swept
Which sin so long foul kept;
The penny's found for which the loser wept.

And, purged with tears,
God's image reappears.
The penny truly shows whose stamp it bears.

The sheep long lost,
Sin's wilderness oft crossed,
Is found, regained, returned. Spare, spare no cost!

'Tis heaven's own suit;
Hark how it woos you to't.
When angels needs must speak, shall man be mute?

JOHN COLLOP

Valediction Forbidding Mourning

As virtuous men pass mildly away,
    And whisper to their souls to go,
Whilst some of their sad friends do say,
    "The breath goes now," and some say "No";

So let us melt and make no noise,
    No tear-floods nor sigh-tempests move;
'Twere profanation of our joys
    To tell the laity our love.

Moving of th' earth brings harms and fears;
    Men reckon what it did and meant;
But trepidation of the spheres,
    Though greater far, is innocent.

Dull sublunary lovers' love
    (Whose soul is sense) cannot admit
Absence, because it doth remove
    Those things which elemented it.

But we by a love so much refined
    That ourselves know not what it is,
Inter-assurèd of the mind,
    Careless eyes, lips, and hands to miss.

Our two souls, therefore, which are one,
  Though I must go, endure not yet
A breach, but an expansion,
  Like gold to airy thinness beat.

If they be two, they are two so
  As stiff twin compasses are two:
Thy soul, the fixt foot, makes no show
  To move, but both do if the other do.

And though it in the center sit,
  Yet when the other far doth roam,
It leans and harkens after it,
  And grows erect as that comes home.

Such wilt thou be to me, who must
  Like th' other foot, obliquely run;
Thy firmness makes my circle just,
  And makes me end, where I begun.

JOHN DONNE

A Noiseless Patient Spider

A noiseless patient spider,
I mark'd where on a little promontory it stood isolated,
Mark'd how to explore the vacant vast surrounding,
It launch'd forth filament, filament, filament, out of itself,
Ever unreeling them, ever tirelessly speeding them.

And you O my soul where you stand,
Surrounded, detached, in measureless oceans of space,
Ceaselessly musing, venturing, throwing, seeking the
   spheres to connect them,
Till the bridge you will need be form'd, till the ductile
   anchor hold,
Till the gossamer thread you fling catch somewhere, O my
   soul.

WALT WHITMAN

The Silken Tent

She is as in a field a silken tent
At midday when a sunny summer breeze
Has dried the dew and all its ropes relent,
So that in guys it gently sways at ease,
And its supporting central cedar pole,
That is its pinnacle to heavenward
And signifies the sureness of the soul,
Seems to owe naught to any single cord,
But strictly held by none, is loosely bound
By countless silken ties of love and thought
To everything on earth the compass round,
And only by one's going slightly taut
In the capriciousness of summer air
Is of the slightest bondage made aware.

ROBERT FROST

No Coward Soul Is Mine

No coward soul is mine,
No trembler in the world's storm-troubled sphere;
 I see Heaven's glories shine,
And faith shines equal, arming me from fear.

O God within my breast,
Almighty, ever-present Deity!
 Life—that in me has rest,
As I—undying Life—have power in Thee!

Vain are the thousand creeds
That move men's hearts—unutterably vain;
 Worthless as withered weeds,
Or idlest froth amid the boundless main,

To waken doubt in one
Holding so fast by Thine infinity;
 So surely anchored on
The steadfast rock of immortality.

With wide-embracing love
Thy spirit animates eternal years
 Pervades and broods above,
Changes, sustains, dissolves, creates, and rears.

Though earth and man were gone,
And suns and universes ceased to be,
   And Thou were left alone,
Every existence would exist in Thee.

   There is not room for Death,
Nor atom that his might could render void;
   Thou—Thou art Being and Breath,
And what Thou art may never be destroyed.

                    EMILY BRONTË

TALES

Casey at the Bat

The outlook wasn't brilliant for the Mudville nine that day;
The score stood four to two, with but one inning more to
   play;
And so, when Cooney died at first, and Barrows did the
   same,
A sickly silence fell upon the patrons of the game.

A straggling few got up to go in deep despair. The rest
Clung to the hope which springs eternal in the human
   breast;
They thought, if only Casey could but get a whack, at that,
They'd put up even money now, with Casey at the bat.

But Flynn preceded Casey, as did also Jimmy Blake,
And the former was a pudding and the latter was a fake;
So upon that stricken multitude grim melancholy sat,
For there seemed but little chance of Casey's getting to the
   bat.

But Flynn let drive a single, to the wonderment of all,
And Blake, the much despised, tore the cover off the ball;
And when the dust had lifted, and they saw what had
   occurred,
There was Jimmy safe on second, and Flynn a-hugging
   third.

Then from the gladdened multitude went up a joyous yell,
It bounded from the mountain-top, and rattled in the dell;
It struck upon the hillside, and recoiled upon the flat;
For Casey, mighty Casey, was advancing to the bat.

There was ease in Casey's manner as he stepped into his
   place,
There was pride in Casey's bearing, and a smile on Casey's
   face;
And when, responding to the cheers, he lightly doffed his
   hat,
No stranger in the crowd could doubt 'twas Casey at the
   bat.

Ten thousand eyes were on him as he rubbed his hands
  with dirt,
Five thousand tongues applauded when he wiped them on
  his shirt;
Then while the writhing pitcher ground the ball into his
  hip,
Defiance gleamed in Casey's eye, a sneer curled Casey's lip.

And now the leather-covered sphere came hurtling
  through the air,
And Casey stood a-watching it in haughty grandeur there;
Close by the sturdy batsman the ball unheeded sped.
"That ain't my style," said Casey. "Strike one," the umpire
  said.

From the benches, black with people, there went a muffled
  roar,
Like the beating of the storm-waves on a stern and distant
  shore;
"Kill him! kill the umpire!" shouted someone on the stand.
And it's likely they'd have killed him had not Casey raised
  his hand.

With a smile of Christian charity great Casey's visage
  shone;
He stilled the rising tumult; he bade the game go on;
He signalled to the pitcher, and once more the spheroid
  flew,
But Casey still ignored it, and the umpire said, "Strike two."

"Fraud!" cried the maddened thousands, and the echo
  answered, "Fraud!"
But a scornful look from Casey, and the audience was awed;
They saw his face grow stern and cold, they saw his
  muscles strain,
And they knew that Casey wouldn't let that ball go by
  again.

The sneer is gone from Casey's lips, his teeth are clenched
  in hate,
He pounds with cruel violence his bat upon the plate;
And now the pitcher holds the ball, and now he lets it go,
And now the air is shattered by the force of Casey's blow.

Oh! somewhere in this favored land the sun is shining
  bright,
The band is playing somewhere, and somewhere hearts are
  light;
And somewhere men are laughing, and somewhere
  children shout,
But there is no joy in Mudville—mighty Casey has struck
  out.

ERNEST LAWRENCE THAYER

Paul Revere's Ride

Listen, my children, and you shall hear
Of the midnight ride of Paul Revere,
On the eighteenth of April, in Seventy-five;
Hardly a man is now alive
Who remembers that famous day and year.

He said to his friend, "If the British march
By land or sea from the town tonight,
Hang a lantern aloft in the belfry arch
Of the North Church tower as a signal light—
One, if by land, and two, if by sea;
And I on the opposite shore will be,
Ready to ride and spread the alarm
Through every Middlesex village and farm,
For the country folk to be up and to arm."

Then he said, "Good night!" and with muffled oar
Silently rowed to the Charlestown shore,
Just as the moon rose over the bay,
Where swinging wide at her moorings lay
The Somerset, British man-of-war;
A phantom ship, with each mast and spar
Across the moon like a prison bar,
And a huge black hulk, that was magnified
By its own reflection in the tide.

Meanwhile, his friend, through alley and street,
Wanders and watches with eager ears,
Till in the silence around him he hears
The muster of men at the barrack door,
The sound of arms, and the tramp of feet,
And the measured tread of the grenadiers,
Marching down to their boats on the shore.

Then he climbed the tower of the Old North Church,
By the wooden stairs, with stealthy tread,
To the belfry-chamber overhead,
And startled the pigeons from their perch
On the somber rafters, that round him made
Masses and moving shapes of shade—
By the trembling ladder, steep and tall,
To the highest window in the wall,
Where he paused to listen and look down
A moment on the roofs of the town,
And the moonlight flowing over all.

Beneath, in the churchyard, lay the dead,
In their night-encampment on the hill,
Wrapped in silence so deep and still
That he could hear, like a sentinel's tread,
The watchful night-wind, as it went
Creeping along from tent to tent,
And seeming to whisper, "All is well!"

A moment only he feels the spell
Of the place and the hour, and the secret dread
Of the lonely belfry and the dead;
For suddenly all his thoughts are bent
On a shadowy something far away,
Where the river widens to meet the bay—
A line of black that bends and floats
On the rising tide, like a bridge of boats.

Meanwhile, impatient to mount and ride,
Booted and spurred, with a heavy stride
On the opposite shore walked Paul Revere.
Now he patted his horse's side,
Now gazed at the landscape far and near,
Then, impetuous, stamped the earth,
And turned and tightened his saddle-girth;
But mostly he watched with eager search
The belfry-tower of the Old North Church,
As it rose above the graves on the hill,
Lonely and spectral and somber and still.
And lo! as he looks, on the belfry's height
A glimmer, and then a gleam of light!
He springs to the saddle, the bridle he turns,
But lingers and gazes, till full on his sight
A second lamp in the belfry burns!

A hurry of hoofs in a village street,
A shape in the moonlight, a bulk in the dark,
And beneath, from the pebbles, in passing, a spark
Struck out by a steed flying fearless and fleet;
That was all! And yet, through the gloom and the light,
The fate of a nation was riding that night;
And the spark struck out by that steed in his flight,
Kindled the land into flame with its heat.

He has left the village and mounted the steep,
And beneath him, tranquil and broad and deep,
Is the Mystic, meeting the ocean tides;
And under the alders that skirt its edge,
Now soft on the sand, now loud on the ledge,
Is heard the tramp of his steed as he rides.

It was twelve by the village clock
When he crossed the bridge into Medford town.
He heard the crowing of the cock,
And the barking of the farmer's dog,
And felt the damp of the river fog,
That rises after the sun goes down.

It was one by the village clock,
When he galloped into Lexington.

He saw the gilded weathercock
Swim in the moonlight as he passed,
And the meeting-house windows, blank and bare,
Gaze at him with a spectral glare,
As if they already stood aghast
At the bloody work they would look upon.

It was two by the village clock,
When he came to the bridge in Concord town.
He heard the bleating of the flock,
And the twitter of birds among the trees,
And felt the breath of the morning breeze
Blowing over the meadows brown.
And one was safe and asleep in his bed
Who at the bridge would be first to fall,
Who that day would be lying dead,
Pierced by a British musket-ball.

You know the rest. In the books you have read,
How the British Regulars fired and fled—
How the farmers gave them ball for ball,
From behind each fence and farmyard wall,
Chasing the redcoats down the lane,
Then crossing the fields to emerge again
Under the trees at the turn of the road,
And only pausing to fire and load.

So through the night rode Paul Revere;
And so through the night went his cry of alarm
To every Middlesex village and farm—
A cry of defiance, and not of fear,
A voice in the darkness, a knock at the door,
And a word that shall echo forevermore!
For, borne on the night-wind of the Past,
Through all our history, to the last,
In the hour of darkness and peril and need,
The people will waken and listen to hear
The hurrying hoofbeats of that steed,
And the midnight message of Paul Revere.

HENRY WADSWORTH LONGFELLOW

Fable

The mountain and the squirrel
Had a quarrel,
And the former called the latter "Little Prig;"
Bun replied,
"You are doubtless very big;
But all sorts of things and weather
Must be taken in together,
To make up a year
And a sphere.
And I think it no disgrace
To occupy my place.
If I'm not so large as you,
You are not so small as I,
And not half so spry.
I'll not deny you make
A very pretty squirrel track;
Talents differ; all is well and wisely put;
If I cannot carry forests on my back,
Neither can you crack a nut."

RALPH WALDO EMERSON

The Raven

Once upon a midnight dreary, while I pondered, weak and
   weary,
Over many a quaint and curious volume of forgotten
   lore,—
While I nodded, nearly napping, suddenly there came a
   tapping,
As of some one gently rapping, rapping at my chamber
   door.
"'Tis some visitor," I muttered, "tapping at my chamber
   door:
     Only this and nothing more."

Ah, distinctly I remember it was in the bleak December,
And each separate dying ember wrought its ghost upon the
   floor.
Eagerly I wished the morrow;—vainly I had sought to
   borrow
From my books surcease of sorrow—sorrow for the lost
   Lenore,
For the rare and radiant maiden whom the angels name
   Lenore:
     Nameless here for evermore.

And the silken sad uncertain rustling of each purple curtain
Thrilled me—filled me with fantastic terrors never felt
  before;
So that now, to still the beating of my heart, I stood
  repeating
" 'Tis some visitor entreating entrance at my chamber door,
Some late visitor entreating entrance at my chamber door:
    This it is and nothing more."

Presently my soul grew stronger; hesitating then no
  longer,
"Sir," said I, "or Madam, truly your forgiveness I implore;
But the fact is I was napping, and so gently you came
  rapping,
And so faintly you came tapping, tapping at my chamber
  door,
That I scarce was sure I heard you"—here I opened wide the
  door:—
    Darkness there and nothing more.

Deep into that darkness peering, long I stood there
  wondering, fearing,
Doubting, dreaming dreams no mortal ever dared to dream
  before;
But the silence was unbroken, and the stillness gave no
  token,
And the only word there spoken was the whispered word,
  "Lenore?"

This I whispered, and an echo murmured back the word,
  "Lenore:"
    Merely this and nothing more.

Back into the chamber turning, all my soul within me
  burning,
Soon again I heard a tapping somewhat louder than before.
"Surely," said I, "surely that is something at my window
  lattice;
Let me see, then, what thereat is, and this mystery explore;
Let my heart be still a moment and this mystery explore:
    'Tis the wind and nothing more."

Open here I flung the shutter, when, with many a flirt and
  flutter,
In there stepped a stately Raven of the saintly days of yore.
Not the least obeisance made he; not a minute stopped or
  stayed he;
But, with mien of lord or lady, perched above my chamber
  door,
Perched upon a bust of Pallas just above my chamber door:
    Perched, and sat, and nothing more.

Then this ebony bird beguiling my sad fancy into smiling
By the grave and stern decorum of the countenance it
     wore,—
"Though thy crest be shorn and shaven, thou," I said, "art
     sure no craven,
Ghastly grim and ancient Raven wandering from the
     Nightly shore:
Tell me what thy lordly name is on the Night's Plutonian
     shore!"
          Quoth the Raven, "Nevermore."

Much I marvelled this ungainly fowl to hear discourse so
     plainly,
Though its answer little meaning—little relevancy bore;
For we cannot help agreeing that no living human being
Ever yet was blessed with seeing bird above his chamber
     door,
Bird or beast upon the sculptured bust above his chamber
     door,
          With such name as "Nevermore."

But the Raven, sitting lonely on the placid bust, spoke only
That one word, as if his soul in that one word he did
     outpour.
Nothing further then he uttered, not a feather then he
     fluttered,
Till I scarcely more than muttered,—"Other friends have
     flown before;

On the morrow *he* will leave me, as my Hopes have flown
   before."
   Then the bird said, "Nevermore."

Startled at the stillness broken by reply so aptly spoken,
"Doubtless," said I, "what it utters is its only stock and
   store,
Caught from some unhappy master whom unmerciful
   Disaster
Followed fast and followed faster till his songs one burden
   bore:
Till the dirges of his Hope that melancholy burden bore
   Of 'Never—nevermore.'"

But the Raven still beguiling my sad fancy into smiling,
Straight I wheeled a cushioned seat in front of bird and bust
   and door;
Then, upon the velvet sinking, I betook myself to linking
Fancy unto fancy, thinking what this ominous bird of yore,
What this grim, ungainly, ghastly, gaunt, and ominous bird
   of yore
   Meant in croaking "Nevermore."

This I sat engaged in guessing, but no syllable expressing
To the fowl whose fiery eyes now burned into my bosom's
   core;

This and more I sat divining, with my head at ease reclining
On the cushion's velvet lining that the lamp-light gloated
    o'er,
But whose velvet violet lining with the lamp-light gloating
    o'er
        She shall press, ah, nevermore!

Then, methought, the air grew denser, perfumed from an
    unseen censer
Swung by seraphim whose foot-falls tinkled on the tufted
    floor.
"Wretch," I cried, "thy God hath lent thee—by these angels
    he hath sent thee
Respite—respite and nepenthe from thy memories of
    Lenore!
Quaff, oh quaff this kind nepenthe, and forget this lost
    Lenore!"
        Quoth the Raven, "Nevermore."

"Prophet!" said I, "thing of evil! prophet still, if bird or devil!
Whether Tempter sent, or whether tempest tossed thee
    here ashore,
Desolate yet all undaunted, on this desert land enchanted—
On this home by Horror haunted—tell me truly, I implore:
Is there—*is* there balm in Gilead?—tell me—tell me,
    I implore!"
        Quoth the Raven, "Nevermore."

"Prophet!" said I, "thing of evil—prophet still, if bird or
    devil!
By that Heaven that bends above us, by that God we both
    adore,
Tell this soul with sorrow laden if, within the distant
    Aidenn,
It shall clasp a sainted maiden whom the angels name
    Lenore:
Clasp a rare and radiant maiden whom the angels name
    Lenore!"
        Quoth the Raven, "Nevermore."

"Be that word our sign of parting, bird or fiend!" I shrieked,
    upstarting:
"Get thee back into the tempest and the Night's Plutonian
    shore!
Leave no black plume as a token of that lie thy soul hath
    spoken!
Leave my loneliness unbroken! quit the bust above my
    door!
Take thy beak from out my heart, and take thy form from
    off my door!"
        Quoth the Raven, "Nevermore."

And the Raven, never flitting, still is sitting, still is sitting
On the pallid bust of Pallas just above my chamber door;
And his eyes have all the seeming of a demon's that is
    dreaming,
And the lamp-light o'er him streaming throws his shadow

on the floor:
And my soul from out that shadow that lies floating on the
floor
Shall be lifted—nevermore!

EDGAR ALLAN POE

A Visit from St. Nicholas

'Twas the night before Christmas, when all through the
  house
Not a creature was stirring, not even a mouse;
The stockings were hung by the chimney with care,
In hopes that St. Nicholas soon would be there;
The children were nestled all snug in their beds,
While visions of sugar-plums danced in their heads;
And mamma in her 'kerchief, and I in my cap,
Had just settled our brains for a long winter's nap,
When out on the lawn there arose such a clatter,
I sprang from the bed to see what was the matter.
Away to the window I flew like a flash,
Tore open the shutters and threw up the sash.
The moon on the breast of the new-fallen snow
Gave the lustre of mid-day to objects below,
When, what to my wondering eyes should appear,
But a miniature sleigh, and eight tiny reindeer,
With a little old driver, so lively and quick,
I knew in a moment it must be St. Nick.
More rapid than eagles his coursers they came,
And he whistled, and shouted, and called them by name;
"Now, Dasher! now, Dancer! now, Prancer and Vixen!
On, Comet! on Cupid! on, Donder and Blitzen!

To the top of the porch! to the top of the wall!
Now dash away! dash away! dash away all!"
As dry leaves that before the wild hurricane fly,
When they meet with an obstacle, mount to the sky,
So up to the house-top the coursers they flew,
With the sleigh full of toys, and St. Nicholas too.
And then, in a twinkling, I heard on the roof
The prancing and pawing of each little hoof.
As I drew in my head, and was turning around,
Down the chimney St. Nicholas came with a bound.
He was dressed all in fur, from his head to his foot,
And his clothes were all tarnished with ashes and soot;
A bundle of toys he had flung on his back,
And he looked like a peddler just opening his pack.
His eyes—how they twinkled—his dimples how merry!
His cheeks were like roses, his nose like a cherry!
His droll little mouth was drawn up like a bow,
And the beard of his chin was as white as the snow;
The stump of a pipe he held tight in his teeth,
And the smoke it encircled his head like a wreath;
He had a broad face and a little round belly,
That shook, when he laughed, like a bowlful of jelly.
He was chubby and plump, a right jolly old elf,
And I laughed when I saw him, in spite of myself;
A wink of his eye and a twist of his head,
Soon gave me to know I had nothing to dread;
He spoke not a word, but went straight to his work,

And filled all the stockings; then turned with a jerk,
And laying his finger aside of his nose,
And giving a nod, up the chimney he rose;
He sprang to his sleigh, to his team gave a whistle,
And away they all flew like the down of a thistle.
But I heard him exclaim, ere he drove out of sight,
"Happy Christmas to all, and to all a good-night."

CLEMENT CLARKE MOORE

TIME

Time

Time is
Too slow for those who Wait,
Too swift for those who Fear,
Too long for those who Grieve,
Too short for those who Rejoice;
But for those who Love
Time is
Eternity.

ANONYMOUS

The Power of Littles

Great events, we often find,
  On little things depend,
And very small beginnings
  Have oft a mighty end.

Letters joined make words,
  And words to books may grow,
As flake on flake descending
  Form an avalanche of snow.

A single utterance may good
  Or evil thought inspire;
One little spark enkindled
  May set a town on fire.

What volumes may be written
  With little drops of ink!
How small a leak, unnoticed,
  A mighty ship will sink!

A tiny insect's labor
  Makes the coral strand,
And mighty seas are girdled
  With grains of golden sand.

A daily penny, saved,
  A fortune may begin;
A daily penny, squandered,
  May lead to vice and sin.

Our life is made entirely
  Of moments multiplied,
As little streamlets, joining,
  Form the ocean's tide.

Our hours and days, our months and years,
  Are in small moments given:
They constitute our time below—
  Eternity in heaven.

ANONYMOUS

Even Such Is Time

Even such is Time, which takes in trust
  Our youth, and joys, and all we have;
And pays us but with age and dust,
  Which, in the dark and silent grave,
When we have wandered all our ways,
Shuts up the story of our days:
  And from which earth and grave and dust
  The Lord shall raise me up, I trust.

SIR WALTER RALEIGH

TRUTH

Truth

Truth is the trial of itself,
   And needs no other touch;
And purer than the purest gold,
   Refine it ne'er so much.

It is the life and light of love,
   The sun that ever shineth,
And spirit of that special grace,
   That faith and love defineth.

It is the warrant of the word,
   That yields a scent so sweet,
As gives a power to faith to tread
   All falsehood under feet.

BEN JONSON

from *An Essay on Criticism*

A little learning is a dangerous thing;
Drink deep, or taste not the Pierian spring:
There shallow draughts intoxicate the brain,
And drinking largely sobers us again.
Fired at first sight with what the Muse imparts,
In fearless youth we tempt the heights of Arts,
While from the bounded level of our mind
Short views we take, nor see the lengths behind;
But more advanced, behold with strange surprise
New distant scenes of endless science rise!
So please at first the towering Alps we try,
Mount o'er the vales, and seem to tread the sky,
The eternal snows appear already past,
And the first clouds and mountains seem the last;
But, those attained, we tremble to survey
The growing labors of the lengthened way,
The increasing prospects tire our wandering eyes,
Hills peep o'er hills, and Alps on Alps arise!

ALEXANDER POPE

Still to Be Neat

Still to be neat, still to be drest
As you were going to a feast;
Still to be powder'd, still perfum'd:
Lady, it is to be presum'd,
Though art's hid causes are not found,
All is not sweet, all is not sound.

Give me a look, give me a face
That makes simplicity a grace;
Robes loosely flowing, hair as free;
Such sweet neglect more taketh me
Than all th' adulteries of art;
They strike mine eyes, but not my heart.

BEN JONSON

VICE

Vice

Vice is a monster of so frightful mien,
As to be hated, needs but to be seen;
Yet seen too oft, familiar with her face,
We first endure, then pity, then embrace.

ALEXANDER POPE

Flattery

'Tis an old maxim in the schools,
That flattery's the food of fools;
Yet now and then your men of wit
Will condescend to take a bit.

JONATHAN SWIFT

Gambling

Of every vice pursued by those
In folly's by-paths rambling,
There's none so bad in its dread close,
As the vile vice of gambling.
It taints our morals, wastes our time
And fills us with vexation.
Destroys our wealth and youthful prime,
And mars our reputation.
Yet I'll aver, with my own eyes,
And I am not called stupid,
I caught sweet Fanny by surprise
A gambling with young Cupid!
Beneath the silent moon's soft beams
In fragrant flowery arbor,
That noted gambling house it seems,
Where players love to harbor.
The cunning god and simple fair,
Sat down to play at leisure
And staked such sums as might impair
A mighty monarch's treasure.
And first they played for locks of hair
And Fanny won the game.
Then cheeks and lips & skin so fair
Her luck was all the same.

Vex'd by the maid to be outdone
Then Cupid made a high bet,
Stak'd all his smiles—a mighty sum
With dimples for a by-bet.
But still she won, & Cupid crost
Made dreadful sad grimaces,
Not only his own smiles he lost,
But all his mother's graces.
Proud Fanny's air and looks and eyes
Of victory gave token,
Her winnings seemed a noble prize,
A bank not to be broken.
Beware sweet girl and go no more
To midnight arbors rambling,
But think how soon you may deplore,
The dreadful end of gambling.
Sly Cupid has but played the knave,
And let you come off winner;
This is the way all gamblers have,
With every new beginner.
Some sharper soon will with you sport,
By Cupid's malice sent hence,
Win all your winnings and leave naught,
But sorrow and repentance.

ROYALL TYLER

The Clod & the Pebble

"Love seeketh not Itself to please,
Nor for itself hath any care;
But for another gives its ease,
And builds a Heaven in Hell's despair."

So sang a little Clod of Clay,
Trodden with the cattle's feet;
But a Pebble of the brook,
Warbled out these metres meet:

"Love seeketh only Self to please,
To bind another to its delight;
Joys in another's loss of ease,
And builds a Hell in Heaven's despite."

WILLIAM BLAKE

Kindly Unhitch That Star, Buddy

I hardly suppose I know anybody who wouldn't rather be a
  success than a failure,
Just as I suppose every piece of crabgrass in the garden
  would much rather be an azalea,
And in celestial circles all the run-of-the-mill angels would
  rather be archangels or at least cherubim and seraphim,
And in the legal world all the little process-servers hope to
  grow up into great big bailiffim and sheriffim.
Indeed, everybody wants to be a wow,
But not everybody knows exactly how.
Some people think they will eventually wear diamonds
  instead of rhinestones
Only by everlastingly keeping their noses to their
  ghrinestones.
And other people think they will be able to put in more time
  at Palm Beach and the Ritz
By not paying too much attention to attendance at the
  office but rather in being brilliant by starts and fits.
Some people after a full day's work sit up all night getting a
  college education by correspondence,
While others seem to think they'll get just as far by
  devoting their evenings to the study of the difference in
  temperament between brunettance and blondance.

Some stake their all on luck,

And others put their faith in their ability to pass the buck.

In short, the world is filled with people trying to achieve
success,

And half of them think they'll get it by saying No and half
of them by saying Yes,

And if all the ones who say No said Yes, and vice versa, such
is the fate of humanity that ninety-nine per cent of them
still wouldn't be any better off than they were before.

Which perhaps is just as well because if everybody was a
success nobody could be contemptuous of anybody else
and everybody would start in all over again trying to be a
bigger success than everybody else so they would have
somebody to be contemptuous of and so on forevermore,

Because when people start hitching their wagons to a star,

That's the way they are.

OGDEN NASH

VIRTUE

Virtue

Sweet day, so cool, so calm, so bright,
The bridal of the earth and sky;
The dew shall weep thy fall tonight,
      For thou must die.

Sweet rose, whose hue, angry and brave,
Bids the rash gazer wipe his eye;
Thy root is ever in its grave,
      And thou must die.

Sweet spring, full of sweet days and roses,
A box where sweets compacted lie;
My music shows ye have your closes,
      And all must die.

Only a sweet and virtuous soul,
Like seasoned timber, never gives;
But though the whole world turn to coal,
    Then chiefly lives.

GEORGE HERBERT

Solitude

Happy the man, whose wish and care
A few paternal acres bound,
Content to breathe his native air
    In his own ground.

Whose herds with milk, whose fields with bread,
Whose flocks supply him with attire;
Whose trees in summer yield him shade,
    In winter, fire.

Blest, who can unconcernedly find
Hours, days, and years slide soft away
In health of body, peace of mind;
    Quiet by day,

Sound sleep by night; study and ease
Together mixed, sweet recreation,
And innocence, which most does please
    With meditation.

Thus let me live, unseen, unknown,
Thus unlamented let me die,
Steal from the world, and not a stone
      Tell where I lie.

ALEXANDER POPE

The Tongue

"The boneless tongue, so small and weak,
Can crush and kill," declared the Greek.

"The tongue destroys a greater horde,"
The Turk asserts, "than does the sword."

A Persian proverb wisely saith,
"A lengthy tongue—an early death."

Or sometimes takes this form instead,
"Don't let your tongue cut off your head."

"The tongue can speak a word whose speed,"
Says the Chinese, "outstrips the steed";

While Arab sages this impart,
"The tongue's great storehouse is the heart."

From Hebrew with the maxim sprung,
"Though feet should slip, ne'er let the tongue."

The sacred writer crown the whole:
"Who keeps the tongue doth keep his soul."

PHILLIPS BURROWS STRONG

Let It Be Forgotten

Let it be forgotten, as a flower is forgotten,
  Forgotten as a fire that once was singing gold,
Let it be forgotten forever and ever,
  Time is a kind friend, he will make us old.

If anyone asks, say it was forgotten
  Long and long ago,
As a flower, as a fire, as a hushed footfall
  In a long forgotten snow.

SARA TEASDALE

VISION

Composed upon Westminster Bridge September 3, 1802

Earth has not anything to show more fair:
Dull would he be of soul who could pass by
A sight so touching in its majesty:
This city now doth, like a garment, wear
The beauty of the morning; silent, bare,
Ships, towers, domes, theaters, and temples lie
Open unto the fields, and to the sky;
All bright and glittering in the smokeless air.
Never did sun more beautifully steep
In his first splendor, valley, rock, or hill;
Ne'er saw I, never felt, a calm so deep!
The river glideth at his own sweet will:
Dear God! the very houses seem asleep;
And all that mighty heart is lying still!

WILLIAM WORDSWORTH

Upon Love

Love brought me to a silent grove,
   And showed me there a tree,
Where some had hanged themselves for love,
   And gave a twist to me.

The halter was of silk and gold,
   That he reached forth unto me:
No otherwise, than if he would
   By dainty things undo me.

He bade me then that necklace use;
   And told me too, he maketh
A glorious end by such a noose,
   His death for love that taketh.

'Twas but a dream; but had I been
   There really alone,
My desperate fears, in love, had seen
   Mine execution.

ROBERT HERRICK

A Dream Within a Dream

Take this kiss upon thy brow!
And, in parting from you now,
Thus much let me avow—
You are not wrong, to deem
That my days have been a dream;
Yet if Hope has flown away
In a night, or in a day,
In a vision, or in none,
Is it therefore the less *gone*?
All that we see or seem
Is but a dream within a dream.

I stand amid the roar
Of a surf-tormented shore,
And I hold within my hand
Grains of the golden sand—
How few! yet how they creep
Through my fingers to the deep,
While I weep—while I weep!
O God! can I not grasp
Them with a tighter clasp?
O God! can I not save
One from the pitiless wave?
Is *all* that we see or seem
But a dream within a dream?

EDGAR ALLAN POE

Our Revels Now Are Ended

(*from* The Tempest)

Our revels now are ended. These our actors,
As I foretold you, were all spirits and
Are melted into air, into thin air:
And, like the baseless fabric of this vision,
The cloud-capp'd towers, the gorgeous palaces,
The solemn temples, the great globe itself,
Yea, all which it inherit, shall dissolve
And, like this insubstantial pageant faded,
Leave not a rack behind. We are such stuff
As dreams are made on, and our little life
Is rounded with a sleep.

WILLIAM SHAKESPEARE

Kubla Khan

In Xanadu did Kubla Khan
   A stately pleasure-dome decree:
Where Alph, the sacred river, ran
Through caverns measureless to man
   Down to a sunless sea.
So twice five miles of fertile ground
With walls and towers were girdled round:
And here were gardens bright with sinuous rills,
Where blossomed many an incense-bearing tree,
And here were forests ancient as the hills,
Enfolding sunny spots of greenery.

But oh! that deep romantic chasm which slanted
Down the green hill athwart a cedarn cover!
A savage place; as holy and enchanted
As e'er beneath a waning moon was haunted
By woman wailing for her demon-lover!
And from this chasm, with ceaseless turmoil seething,
As if this earth in fast thick pants were breathing,
A mighty fountain momently was forced,
Amid whose swift half-intermitted burst
Huge fragments vaulted like rebounding hail,
Or chaffy grain beneath the thresher's flail:
And 'mid these dancing rocks at once and ever
It flung up momently the sacred river.

Five miles meandering with a mazy motion
Through wood and dale the sacred river ran,
Then reached the caverns measureless to man,
And sank in tumult to a lifeless ocean:
And 'mid this tumult Kubla heard from far
Ancestral voices prophesying war!

   The shadow of the dome of pleasure
   Floated midway on the waves;
   Where was heard the mingled measure
   From the fountain and the caves.
It was a miracle of rare device,
A sunny pleasure-dome with caves of ice!

   A damsel with a dulcimer
   In a vision once I saw:
   It was an Abyssinian maid,
   And on her dulcimer she played,
   Singing of Mount Abora.
   Could I revive within me
   Her symphony and song,
   To such a deep delight 'twould win me,
That with music loud and long,
I would build that dome in air,
That sunny dome! those caves of ice!
And all who heard should see them there,
And all should cry, Beware! Beware!

His flashing eyes, his floating hair!
Weave a circle round him thrice,
And close your eyes with holy dread,
For he on honey-dew hath fed,
And drunk the milk of Paradise.

SAMUEL TAYLOR COLERIDGE

Ode to a Nightingale

My heart aches, and a drowsy numbness pains
  My sense, as though of hemlock I had drunk,
Or emptied some dull opiate to the drains
  One minute past, and Lethe-wards had sunk:
'Tis not through envy of thy happy lot,
  But being too happy in thy happiness,—
    That thou, light-winged Dryad of the trees,
      In some melodious plot
  Of beechen green, and shadows numberless,
  Singest of summer in full-throated ease.

O for a draught of vintage, that hath been
  Cooled a long age in the deep-delved earth,
Tasting of Flora and the country green,
  Dance, and Provençal song, and sun-burnt mirth
O for a beaker full of the warm South,
  Full of the true, the blushful Hippocrene,
    With beaded bubbles winking at the brim,
      And purple-stained mouth;
That I might drink, and leave the world unseen
  And with thee fade away into the forest dim:

Fade far away, dissolve, and quite forget
    What thou among the leaves hast never known,
The weariness, the fever, and the fret
    Here, where men sit and hear each other groan;
Where palsy shakes a few, sad, last gray hairs,
    When youth grows pale, and spectre-thin, and dies;
        Where but to think is to be full of sorrow
            And leaden-eyed despairs;
Where beauty cannot keep her lustrous eyes,
    Or new love pine at them beyond tomorrow.

Away! away! for I will fly to thee,
    Not charioted by Bacchus and his pards,
But on the viewless wings of Poesy,
    Though the dull brain perplexes and retards:
Already with thee! tender is the night,
    And haply the Queen-Moon is on her throne,
        Clustered around by all her starry fays;
            But here there is no light,
    Save what from heaven is with the breezes blown
        Through verdurous glooms and winding mossy ways.

I cannot see what flowers are at my feet,
  Nor what soft incense hangs upon the boughs,
But, in embalmed darkness, guess each sweet
  Wherewith the seasonable month endows
The grass, the thicket, and the fruit-tree wild;
  White hawthorn, and the pastoral eglantine;
    Fast-fading violets covered up in leaves;
      And mid-May's eldest child,
  The coming musk-rose, full of dewy wine,
    The murmurous haunt of flies on summer eves.

Darkling I listen; and for many a time
  I have been half in love with easeful Death,
Called him soft names in many a mused rhyme,
  To take into the air my quiet breath;
Now more than ever seems it rich to die,
  To cease upon the midnight with no pain,
    While thou art pouring forth thy soul abroad
      In such an ecstasy!
  Still wouldst thou sing, and I have ears in vain—
    To thy high requiem become a sod.

Thou wast not born for death, immortal Bird!
  No hungry generations tread thee down;
The voice I hear this passing night was heard
  In ancient days by emperor and clown:

Perhaps the self-same song that found a path
   Through the sad heart of Ruth, when, sick for home
      She stood in tears amid the alien corn;
         The same that oft-times hath
      Charmed magic casements, opening on the foam
         Of perilous seas, in faery lands forlorn.

Forlorn! the very word is like a bell
   To toll me back from thee to my sole self!
Adieu! the fancy cannot cheat so well
   As she is famed to do, deceiving elf.
Adieu! adieu! thy plaintive anthem fades
   Past the near meadows, over the still stream,
      Up the hill-side; and now 'tis buried deep
         In the next valley-glades:
      Was it a vision, or a waking dream?
         Fled is that music:—do I wake or sleep?

JOHN KEATS

WAR

The Glories of Our Blood and State

The glories of our blood and state
  Are shadows, not substantial things;
There is no armour against fate;
  Death lays his icy hand on kings:
    Sceptre and Crown
    Must tumble down,
And in the dust be equal made
With the poor crookèd scythe and spade.

Some men with swords may reap the field,
  And plant fresh laurels where they kill:
But their strong nerves at last must yield;
  They tame but one another still:
    Early or late
    They stoop to fate,
And must give up their murmuring breath,
When they, pale captives, creep to death.

The garlands wither on your brow,
   Then boast no more your mighty deeds;
Upon Death's purple altar now
   See, where the victor-victim bleeds:
      Your heads must come
      To the cold tomb;
Only the actions of the just
Smell sweet, and blossom in their dust.

JAMES SHIRLEY

YOUTH

Nothing Gold Can Stay

Nature's first green is gold,
Her hardest hue to hold.
Her early leaf's a flower;
But only so an hour.
Then leaf subsides to leaf.
So Eden sank to grief,
So dawn goes down to day.
Nothing gold can stay.

ROBERT FROST

Good-bye My Fancy!

Good-bye my Fancy!
Farewell dear mate, dear love!
I'm going away, I know not where,
Or to what fortune, or whether I may ever see you again,
So good-bye my Fancy.

Now for my last—let me look back a moment;
The slower fainter ticking of the clock is in me,
Exit, nightfall, and soon the heart-thud stopping.

Long have we lived, joy'd, caress'd together;
Delightful!—now separation—Good-bye my Fancy.

Yet let me not be too hasty,
Long indeed have we lived, slept, filter'd, become really
    blended into one;
Then if we die we die together, (yes, we'll remain one,)
If we go anywhere we'll go together to meet what happens,
May-be we'll be better off and blither, and learn something,
May-be it is yourself now really ushering me to the true
    songs, (who knows?)
May-be it is you the mortal knob really undoing, turning—
    so now finally,
Good-bye—and hail! my Fancy.

WALT WHITMAN

INDEXES

INDEX OF FIRST LINES

INDEX OF AUTHORS

INDEX OF TITLES

Acknowledgments

Thanks to the following publishers for their permission to reprint the poems listed:

AMONG SCHOOL CHILDREN, SAILING TO BYZANTIUM, and WHEN YOU ARE OLD reprinted with permission of Macmillan Publishing Company and A. P. Watt Limited on behalf of Michael B. Yeats and Macmillan London Ltd. from *The Poems of W. B. Yeats: A New Edition*, edited by Richard J. Finneran. Copyright 1928 by Macmillan Publishing Company, renewed 1956 by Georgie Yeats.

AND DEATH SHALL HAVE NO DOMINION, and DO NOT GO GENTLE INTO THAT GOOD NIGHT by Dylan Thomas from *Poems of Dylan Thomas*. Copyright 1943 by New Directions Publishing Corporation, 1952 by Dylan Thomas. Reprinted by permission of New Directions Publishing Corporation and David Higham Associates Limited.

ANYONE LIVED IN A PRETTY HOW TOWN is reprinted from *Complete Poems, 1913–1962*, by e. e. cummings, by permission of Liveright Publishing Corporation. Copyright © 1923, 1925, 1931, 1935, 1938, 1939, 1940, 1944, 1945, 1946, 1947, 1948, 1949, 1950, 1951, 1952, 1953, 1954, 1955, 1956, 1957, 1958, 1959, 1960, 1961, 1962 by the Trustees for the e. e. cummings Trust. Copyright © 1961, 1963, 1968 by Marion Morehouse Cummings.

APPRAISAL reprinted with permission of Macmillan Publishing Company from *Collected Poems* by Sara Teasdale. Copyright 1926 by Macmillan Publishing Company, renewed 1954 by Mamie T. Wheless.

ARS POETICA from *Collected Poems 1917–1982* by Archibald MacLeish. Copyright © 1955 by Houghton Mifflin Company. Copyright © 1983 by Houghton Mifflin Company, Brinton P. Roberts, Esquire and G. D'Andelot Belin, Esquire. Reprinted by permission of Houghton Mifflin Company.

DIRGE WITHOUT MUSIC, and PITY ME NOT by Edna St. Vincent Millay. From *Collected Poems*, Harper & Row. Copyright © 1923, 1928, 1951, 1955 by Edna St. Vincent Millay and Norma Millay Ellis. Reprinted by permission.